IT AIN'T SAUCE, IT'S GRAVY

IT AIN'T SAUCE,
IT'S GRAVY

MACARONI, HOMESTYLE CHEESESTEAKS,

THE BEST MEATBALLS IN THE WORLD,

AND HOW FOOD SAVED MY LIFE

STEVE MARTORANO

WITH MICHAEL RUBINO

 ALFRED A. KNOPF | NEW YORK | 2014

THIS IS A BORZOI BOOK PUBLISHED BY ALFRED A. KNOPF

www.aaknopf.com

Knopf, Borzoi Books, and the colophon are registered trademarks
of Random House LLC.

Portions of this work first appeared in *Yo Cuz*, copyright © 2011 by Steve Martorano,
published by Northstar Books, Indianapolis, in 2011.

Cataloging-in-Publication Data is available from the Library of Congress.
ISBN 978-0-385-34989-5
ISBN 978-0-385-534990-1 (eBook)

Food photography by Carlos Beauchamp
Jacket photographs by Carlos Beauchamp
Jacket design by Abby Weintraub

Manufactured in China

First Edition

I would like to dedicate this book

to my late dear friend and attorney, Ed Lassman.

If it weren't for him,

none of this would have been possible.

YO CUZ!

CONTENTS

IT AIN'T SAUCE, IT'S GRAVY

YO CUZ!

INTRODUCTION

IT'S NO SMALL MIRACLE you're reading this book.

I could've been a gangster. I should've driven a delivery truck. I would've ended up dead or broke had I joined either the family business or The Family Business; there was a fine line between the two when I came of age in a South Philadelphia row home during the 1970s and 1980s.

But I'm the kind of guy who believes that when you run into a dead end, you look for a detour. Yeah, taking the long way around can be a pain in the ass, but you may be surprised at where you end up. I know I am.

Almost thirty-five years ago, I started that journey when I began selling sandwiches out of my mother's basement. Today, I have five restaurants where I cook Italian-American food South Philly-style, a line of jarred sauces, a wine label, and an inspirational jewelry-and-clothing collection. I've cooked on TV for people like Jimmy Kimmel, Paula Deen, and Mo'Nique. Hundreds of celebrities and professional athletes—some of my all-time favorites—have come into my restaurants and enjoyed my food.

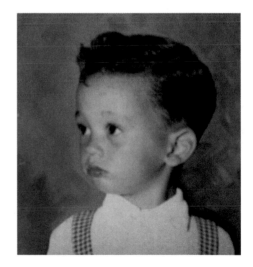

For a guy from the neighborhood, I've done all right. I really didn't dream of anything like this. But maybe my mother, Lillian, did. She's the one who gave me a head start in the kitchen and a love of great food. The saying goes that a person begins as a gleam in his father's eye, right? Me? I began as a rumbling in my mother's stomach. When she was pregnant with me, she craved macaroni seven days a week.

Take note: In Philly, we call it *macaroni*, not pasta. And, cuz, it ain't sauce–it's *gravy*. The *cuz* thing? That's

ABOVE *Baby Steven*
TOP, LEFT *Mo'Nique, Marsha, my girl-friend, and me*
TOP, CENTER *Jimmy Kimmel*
TOP, RIGHT *Paula Deen*

just our way of saying, "I don't remember or know your name, but you seem like a good guy, and chances are we're probably related—cousins or something." It means, "You're one of us." Even if the people I hung out with in South Philly weren't all really related, it *seemed* that way. After all, among my friends and neighbors, the weekly menu was a shared ritual that pretty much never changed, regardless of the weather or the season.

Every Monday, your mother would make a pot of soup, like chicken or oxtail. On Tuesday, we had the leftover gravy from Sunday with a different type of macaroni. (Rigatoni tasted different from fusilli. Fusilli tasted different from perciatelli.) Wednesdays were for chicken or veal cutlets with ketchup on the side, chicken-flavored Rice-A-Roni, and a salad. On Thursday, we had macaroni again. On Friday, it was linguine and clams, peppers and eggs, or tuna-fish salad with hard-boiled eggs and sliced tomato. Never any meat. It was a Catholic thing. On Saturday, your mom didn't cook; it was her day off. Saturday was always pizza, or we ate takeout like cheesesteaks, or cold cuts.

In Philly, we call it *macaroni*, not pasta. And, cuz, it ain't sauce—it's *gravy*.

But Sundays were the best. On Sunday in South Philly, you always heard someone say, "What time do you want me to put the water on?" This referred to the pot of water used to cook the macaroni. Rigatoni was my favorite. Every Sunday, my mother would make rigatoni and put the leftovers in the refrigerator. Late at night, I'd go downstairs, take out the bowl of macaroni, pour a glass of homemade iced tea, watch some TV, and then head back to bed. Even cold macaroni right out of the refrigerator was delicious; that's how I knew my mother was a great cook.

Sundays started early. You didn't even need an alarm clock—we had meatballs for that. Maybe you would wake up after staying out late on a Saturday night, maybe you still had a little buzz, and—*oh, shit!*—it would hit you. You'd hear the meat sizzling, smell the tomatoes with the garlic, olive oil, and the pork. Forget about eating bacon and eggs in our house. Hangover or not, you wanted to get your ass out of bed to get to that plate of fried meatballs.

And my mother's gravy? Get outta here—it was phenomenal. Every Sunday, she made a pot of gravy that contained pigs' feet, pork skin, ribs, sausage, braciole, and especially meatballs. Some people baked their meatballs, some people threw them right into the pot, but we fried ours first. Before the meatballs went into the gravy, we'd tear through a dozen

or so of them. My mother would always yell, "Stop! There won't be any left for dinner." I couldn't argue with that, but later in the day I'd sneak back into the kitchen and make a gravy sandwich: sliced Italian bread, gravy, grated cheese. The best things are usually the simplest things.

People don't really do this anymore, but back then, we made it a point to eat as a family. A really big family. My mother, father, grandparents, aunts, uncles, and, of course, cousins—my best friends. In my family, like the others I knew, they fed you and fed you. It was the way we showed love. Food was always part of the equation, always the solution to a problem, always a way to mark an occasion. Any occasion. Someone got married, there was food. Someone died, there was food. You didn't feel good, there was food. The only way you got skinny was if you went to prison. It was like the South Philly version of Weight Watchers or something.

My philosophy today comes from the tradition of those great family meals, and it remains pretty simple. I'm a cook—just like you. I mean that. I'm not a chef. I didn't go to school for this. I don't have any special training. There isn't any magic formula. Most of what I learned, I got from my mother and Gram and the other members of my family. Basically, I cook what they cooked; the only difference is that today I use the best ingredients I can find. Both of my parents worked for little pay when I was a kid, so we couldn't afford that kind of quality. Great meals just become better with top-notch ingredients.

At its heart, Italian cooking—or at least Italian-American cooking—is really peasant cooking. You don't have to have a

TOP *Family dinner at 6th and Fitzwater*
ABOVE *Me and Gram*

million dollars to put great food on the table. Another thing I've learned is that there's no right or wrong. Want more garlic? Great! You love cheese? Add more. Cook what you love. I picked up on that as I got more interested in cooking and started trying different kinds of food and going to different restaurants. I'd try to learn how to replicate the dishes I liked and just shake my head at the ones I didn't. Either certain flavors work for you or they don't—don't fight your instincts. Food, like romance, is very personal and subjective.

Since my parents often worked long hours, that gave me a chance to mess around in the kitchen and cook for myself. Like a lot of beginners, I started off with eggs—maybe adding peppers or some cheese or whatever we might have in the fridge. And my interest just kind of took off from there.

Honestly, though, my career in food almost didn't happen. I'm proud to be from South Philly and I treasure my family—they're everything to me. But sometimes, if you're not careful, those things—the pressure to be a certain way because of where you're from or who you're related to—can become a kind of prison. I know this from experience.

My mother worked at a company that made bathing suits, one of my grandmothers ran numbers (a weekly neighborhood lottery, except it was, um, an illegal one), and my father, Joe, was a part-time loan shark. (When I bought my first car, he loaned me the money. I had to pay it all back—plus the points. He didn't mess around.)

His primary job, though, was at John's Vending, the biggest business of its kind in Philadelphia. Two of his brothers, John and Raymond, owned the place, and the rest of the family worked there. My cousin Carol, Aunt Philly's daughter, helped run the company. She is like the sister I never had—very loyal. Today, she's the one who helps keep this family together, just like my paternal grandmother once did. John's Vending supplied cigarettes, cigarette machines, pinball machines, and jukeboxes all across Pennsylvania and parts of New Jer-

TOP *My mom, Lil, and dad, Joe, at a family function*
ABOVE *My cousin Carol, my dad feeding me, and my cousin George*

sey. I grew up loving R&B and Motown music, because my father would bring home old 45 vinyl.

He drove a truck for a living, and that's what everyone probably thought I was going to do, too. The kids at school even called me "Stevie Truck" back then, and, even today, some still know me by that nickname. Not much was expected of me by either my family or the people I grew up with. And who could blame them? I hated school and got bad grades, so going to college wasn't an option.

The vending company was our family business, but one of John's Vending's most interesting employees ran a different kind of "family" enterprise. Philadelphia mob boss Angelo Bruno was, for a long time, a salesman for the company. During his reign (1959–1980), the Philly mob grew in notoriety, making Bruno one of the top Mafia leaders in the United States. Nicknamed the "Docile Don" or "Gentle Don," he allowed very little violence during his reign. Some said his old-world ways caused him to miss opportunities in narcotics and in Las Vegas, but he was able to gain control over the emerging gambling empire of Atlantic City.

Angelo Bruno was a very close friend and associate of my uncle Raymond, the oldest of my father's brothers. If you saw Angelo walking in the neighborhood, my uncle was almost always stride for stride with him. If Angelo crawled, Uncle Raymond was right there, too. So—my other option was to work for Uncle Raymond. I had nothing but respect for that man, and most everyone I knew felt the same—working for him would have been an honor. At one point, I was headed in that direction: I did a little bit of this and a little of that, and got into my fair share of trouble. I stole a couple of cars that I took to a chop shop, and once even tried my hand at selling drugs. (That lasted for, like, five minutes.) It was really stupid stuff, but I was looking for options, a way to get respect or money or both. Looking back on that period in my life, I see that those mistakes I made got me neither.

But, at a certain point, I realized that both of my options really weren't options at all. Either I was going to die of a heart attack at an early age after working my balls off, like my father; or, like other guys I hung out with, I was going to go to prison—or worse.

One night in 1981, a buddy named Joey and I were at a South Philly

ABOVE *Grandmom Mary and my uncle Raymond Martorano*

cheesesteak joint when a panic broke out. As we were ordering, two guys ran past us—and then a third. We grabbed the last guy and he started yelling, "They just blew up Phil Testa's house!" We threw down our money, got our cheesesteaks, and followed the crowd.

Testa was the boss of the Philly mob, a close family friend, and father to my friend Salvie. The former boss, Angelo Bruno, had been assassinated by some of his own men almost a year earlier. After a period of uncertainty, Testa had been picked as Bruno's successor from a group of men that included my uncle Raymond. Then the shit really hit the fan, and guys started turning up dead left and right. We were used to violence in South Philly, but nothing like we saw when we arrived at Testa's Girard Estates home in South Philly. It was the beginning of a mob war.

We got there just before the cops and EMTs, but there was nothing we could do except watch in disbelief. A crowd had gathered in the cold on the dark street in front of the neighborhood's nicest home. People running. People standing. People sitting on the curb. They were in a daze, the whole neighborhood—crying and whispering.

They say the grass is always greener on the other side of the fence. I say my side is concrete.

It was March, but it smelled like the Fourth of July. Steam rose off the metal bits that covered the ground. Soon the scene was flooded with lights from police cars and paddy wagons. Parts of Testa, some of his clothes, and his personal belongings were scattered all over the park across the street.

When we saw what was left of Testa, the whispering turned into screaming.

"What the fuck is happening in Philly?" someone cried.

"Jesus Christ, another boss?" I thought as I grabbed a spot on the curb and unwrapped my cheesesteak, still warm but soggy.

What the fuck *is* happening? I wondered. And who would be next? My uncle? There wasn't going to be any retirement to a nice house on the hill for a guy like him, that was for sure. In his line of work, you didn't retire—either it was life in jail or you got whacked. If I followed in that path, how was I going to avoid the same fate?

I took a bite of my cheesesteak and watched the craziness in front of me. I had so many questions. I didn't know it at the time, but the answer was in my hand.

That's the day I started to figure things out; I eventually decided I couldn't let my circumstances—family, friends, and environment—dictate who I was or what I could become.

Obviously, South Philly is a big part of me—that will never, ever change. And on some level, you'll see and feel that when you have dinner at one of my restaurants: the food you eat; the music you hear; the movies you watch; and, yeah, sometimes even the attitude you encounter. (Hey, like it says on my menus: DON'T BREAK BALLS!) I left the neighborhood, but the neighborhood never left me.

Everything I do is a reflection of those two things: family and neighborhood.

The same goes with family—only deeper.

Everything I do is a reflection of those two things: family and neighborhood. You might not realize it, but there's a part of me in each dish I serve, whether it's a great memory, a funny story, a failure, or an ambition. Eating at one of my restaurants is kind of like reading my autobiography.

So—how did I get here? Sometimes I'm not entirely sure, but I do know this: food saved me. And even though you probably bought this book for the meatball recipe, do me a favor and stick around for the stories. After all, there wouldn't be one without the other.

YO CUZ!

SALADS, SANDWICHES, AND ANTIPASTI

MARTORANO SALAD

SERVES 4

Whenever we had macaroni as kids, I had a salad on the side. And we had macaroni a lot—every Sunday, Tuesday, and Thursday. One thing I've learned since then is that **you don't need expensive red-wine vinegar to make a great dressing.** Red-wine vinegar, by nature, is meant to be an inexpensive product. Put your money to better use by buying a great olive oil. Laudemio, Olio Verde, and Badia a Coltibuono are some of my favorites. You can find these in Italian specialty stores, great supermarkets, or online.

One romaine heart

1 pint grape tomatoes, halved

¼ cup julienned red onion

½ cup peeled and chopped American cucumber

⅓ cup extra-virgin olive oil

⅓ cup red-wine vinegar

Kosher salt and freshly ground black pepper to taste

Granulated garlic to taste

3 ounces Parmigiano Reggiano

Cut the romaine heart into quarters lengthwise, and then across into 1-inch pieces. In a bowl, toss the lettuce, tomatoes, red onion, cucumber, olive oil, and vinegar, mixing until all the lettuce is coated. Season the salad with salt, pepper, and granulated garlic. With a peeler, slice the cheese and place on top of the salad. Serve family-style.

VEAL CUTLET INSALATA

SERVES 4

Veal can be expensive, and finding a good cut in the supermarket can be a challenge. **But here's a secret: lots of restaurants will sell you veal but actually serve you pork instead.** That's bullshit—it's no way to run a business—but it isn't a bad idea if you're trying to save on your grocery bill at home. Give it a shot and see if you can tell the difference.

Four 3-ounce slices veal tenderloin, pounded thin

Granulated garlic to taste

Kosher salt and freshly ground black pepper to taste

¼ cup all-purpose flour

¾ cup vegetable oil

EGG WASH

3 eggs

½ teaspoon kosher salt

½ teaspoon freshly ground black pepper

¼ cup finely chopped fresh Italian parsley

¼ cup grated Parmigiano Reggiano

BREAD-CRUMB MIXTURE

2 cups unseasoned bread crumbs

¼ cup finely chopped fresh Italian parsley

¼ cup grated Parmigiano Reggiano

1 recipe Martorano Salad (page 15)

4 ounces Parmigiano Reggiano, shaved

TO MAKE THE EGG WASH Crack the eggs into a medium bowl and add the salt, pepper, parsley, and cheese. Whisk together until well blended. In a separate bowl, mix the bread crumbs, parsley, and cheese until they are well combined. Set both bowls aside.

On a plate, season the veal on both sides with granulated garlic, salt, and pepper. Dredge the tenderloin in the flour, shaking off the excess. Dip the tenderloin into the egg wash, and then coat in the bread-crumb mixture. Heat the vegetable oil in a large sauté pan, and carefully add the veal, frying one piece at a time, until both sides are golden brown. Divide the cooked veal and Martorano Salad among four plates. Shave Parmigiano Reggiano on top of the veal, and enjoy.

VEAL PARMESAN SANDWICH

SERVES 4

This is a straightforward Italian-American classic, and it's always one of the most popular items in my restaurants. A lot of the veal you find in stores and restaurants comes from the top of the round, but you never know what you're going to get: sometimes it's tender, sometimes it's not. **I only use the tenderloin, because you're guaranteed a great piece of meat.** It's like cutting into butter.

Four 3-ounce slices veal tenderloin, pounded thin

Kosher salt and freshly ground black pepper to taste

Granulated garlic to taste

¼ cup all-purpose flour

¾ cup vegetable oil

EGG WASH

3 eggs

½ teaspoon kosher salt

½ teaspoon freshly ground black pepper

¼ cup finely chopped fresh Italian parsley

¼ cup grated Parmigiano Reggiano

BREAD-CRUMB MIXTURE

2 cups unseasoned bread crumbs

¼ cup finely chopped fresh Italian parsley

¼ cup grated Parmigiano Reggiano

4 Italian hoagie rolls

3 cups Sunday Pork Gravy (page 78)

2 ounces Parmigiano Reggiano, grated, plus more for serving

1 pound Fresh Mozzarella (page 29), thinly sliced

TO MAKE THE EGG WASH Crack the eggs into a medium bowl, and add the salt, pepper, parsley, and cheese. Whisk together until well blended. In a separate bowl, mix the bread crumbs, parsley, and cheese until well combined. Set aside. On a plate, season the veal on both sides with salt, pepper, and granulated garlic. Dredge the tenderloin in the flour, shaking off the excess. Dip the tenderloin into the egg wash, and then coat in the bread-crumb mixture. Heat the vegetable oil in a large sauté pan, and carefully add the veal, frying one piece at a time until both sides are golden brown. Next, heat your oven to 350 degrees F, and slice the rolls three-quarters of the way through, lengthwise. Take the cooked veal and cut it in half lengthwise. Place the veal on a pan or sheet pan, cover with gravy, and sprinkle with Parmigiano Reggiano. Top the veal with slices of fresh mozzarella until it is covered, and place in the oven. When the cheese is halfway cooked, place the rolls in the oven and allow to crisp up.

To assemble the sandwiches, place each half of a tenderloin inside of a roll, and garnish with freshly grated Parmigiano Reggiano.

ITALIAN HOAGIE

SERVES 4

I got my big break selling hoagies like this one. The sandwich itself goes by a bunch of other names—grinder, sub, poor boy, hero—but in Philly we call it a hoagie. Supposedly, the name came about around World War I, when Italian immigrants used to bring their lunch—huge sandwiches—to work at the shipyards on Hog Island. Workers started calling the sandwiches "hoggies," but over time they ended up being called hoagies. **I serve mine with Italian long hots,** which are fried hot peppers. You can find these jarred in Italian specialty stores and most groceries.

ROASTED PEPPERS

2 red bell peppers

2 yellow bell peppers

2 tablespoons extra-virgin olive oil

2 tablespoons coarsely chopped fresh Italian parsley

½ teaspoon kosher salt

½ teaspoon freshly ground black pepper

½ teaspoon granulated garlic

4 Italian hoagie rolls

4 ounces prosciutto di Parma, thinly sliced

4 ounces sharp provolone, thinly sliced

4 leaves from romaine heart

4 Italian long hots

2 tablespoons torn fresh basil

Pinch of dried oregano

¼ cup extra-virgin olive oil

TO MAKE THE ROASTED PEPPERS Preheat a grill to 350 degrees F. Place the whole peppers on the grill and roast them till the skin crisps, rotating them so all sides of the peppers become fully black. Place the peppers in a bowl, cover with plastic wrap, and let the peppers steam for 5 minutes; this will allow the skin to come off more easily. When the peppers are cool to the touch, take a cloth and wipe the skin off the peppers. Do not run the peppers under water: this will take away all the flavor. After the skins have been removed, cut the peppers in half lengthwise and remove the stems and seeds. Cut the peppers into quarters, giving you eight pieces per pepper.

Place the peppers in a bowl, and add the olive oil, parsley, salt, black pepper, and granulated garlic; set aside.

Preheat your oven to 350 degrees F. Cut each Italian roll three-quarters of the way through, lengthwise, and bake open-faced for 5 minutes. Remove the bread from the oven, and start to assemble the sandwiches. Layer the rolls first with the prosciutto, then follow with the provolone cheese, the romaine leaves, and the roasted peppers. Top each sandwich with an Italian long hot, some basil and oregano, and a drizzle of olive oil.

SOUTH PHILLY CHEESESTEAK

SERVES 4

If you know anything about South Philly food, you know the cheesesteak. There are a lot of great places that make great steaks, but **if you ask me, my mom made the best.** This is how she did it.

1 yellow onion

2 tablespoons extra-virgin olive oil

1 pound beef rib-eye meat, thinly sliced

Pinch of kosher salt

Pinch of freshly ground black pepper

Pinch of granulated garlic

6 ounces white American cheese, sliced

4 Italian hoagie rolls

4 vinegar hot cherry peppers

NOTE *Ask your local butcher to slice the rib-eye thinly.*

TO PREPARE THE ONION Peel the skin, and cut the onion into 1-inch chunks. In a medium sauté pan, heat the olive oil and cook the onion over medium-low heat for 10 to 15 minutes, until the pieces are tender and have turned a caramel color. Set aside.

Season the sliced rib-eye with the salt, pepper, and granulated garlic, and set aside. Heat a large sauté pan and add the cooked onions and seasoned rib-eye. With two spoons, pull the meat apart as it cooks. Continue to pull the meat apart and cook until it is no longer pink. Next add the sliced white American cheese, cover the pan, and allow the cheese to melt on top of the meat. Then mix the cheese into the meat.

Preheat your oven to 375 degrees F. Get the crustiest and freshest Italian hoagie rolls your local bakery has. Slice them three-quarters of the way through, lengthwise. You can take out some of the bread inside the roll to get a better meat-to-bread ratio. Place the hoagies in the oven, and bake for 5 minutes. This will make the rolls hot and crusty. Carefully take the rolls out of the oven, and divide the cheesesteak meat evenly among the rolls. Slice the sandwiches in half, and garnish with hot cherry peppers.

VARIATION

TO MAKE IT PIZZAIOLA-STYLE Slice beefsteak tomatoes ¼ inch thick (one tomato will give you four or five slices). Season the tomatoes with salt, pepper, granulated garlic, chopped fresh basil, and extra-virgin olive oil. Add the tomatoes to the meat mixture while the cheese is melting, and season with dried oregano.

NOTE *August through September, the best tomatoes are Jersey tomatoes.*

ROAST PORK SANDWICH (Italian Dip)

SERVES 4

Salvie Testa was a dear friend of mine who was a capo under mob boss Nicky Scarfo. Salvie was murdered a few years after his father, former mob boss Phil Testa, was killed in an explosion. Supposedly, Scarfo was responsible for both deaths. Salvie was known as a violent person (rumor had it that he was involved in more than fifteen hits), but I never saw that side of him. He was a regular at Anton's, a bar that my father ran and where I first started to cook. **Salvie loved my roast-pork sandwiches.** When I make them today, I think of him.

3 pounds pork butt, deboned and trussed

1 tablespoon kosher salt

1 tablespoon freshly ground black pepper

1 tablespoon granulated garlic

3 stalks celery, cut into ⅓-inch pieces

2 carrots, cut into ¼-inch pieces

1 medium yellow onion, cut into ¼-inch pieces

3 cups chicken stock

SAUCE

6 cups chicken stock

Drippings from the pan

3 bay leaves, dried

8 vinegar cherry peppers, with juice

1 tablespoon granulated garlic

4 Italian hoagie rolls

Broccoli rabe (recipe follows)

4 ounces sharp provolone, thinly sliced

Preheat the oven to 350 degrees F. Season the pork butt with the salt, pepper, and granulated garlic. In a 4-inch-deep roasting pan, arrange the celery, carrots, and onion in the center, making a bed for the pork. Place the seasoned pork on top of the vegetables, and add the chicken stock. Place in the oven, and cook for 2½ hours, or until the center of the pork reaches 145 degrees F. Remove the pork from the oven, and allow it to cool in the refrigerator for 2 hours. (Doing this will prevent the pork from shredding when it is sliced.) Strain the vegetables from the stock, and discard. Reserve the liquid. When the roast is cool, you can use a knife or bring to your butcher to slice.

TO MAKE THE SAUCE in a pot, combine the chicken stock, the liquid from your roasting pan, the bay leaves, the vinegar peppers with their squeezed-out juice, and the granulated garlic. Place over medium heat, and allow to reduce by half.

TO MAKE THE SANDWICHES Dip the sliced pork into the pot of sauce, and heat through. Slice the hoagie rolls lengthwise, add pork and broccoli rabe, and top with slices of sharp provolone cheese.

BROCCOLI RABE

2 tablespoons extra-virgin olive oil

4 fresh garlic cloves, whole

2 anchovy fillets, whole

One bunch broccoli rabe

½ cup chicken stock

¼ teaspoon crushed red-pepper flakes

Heat a sauté pan with the olive oil, brown the garlic, and add the anchovies. Cut off the woody parts of the stems and place the broccoli rabe in the pan, add the chicken stock and red-pepper flakes, and cook for 4 minutes, or until the broccoli rabe is tender.

PEPPER-AND-EGG SANDWICH

SERVES 4

When my uncle Raymond was in prison, I used to make him pepper-and-egg sandwiches and sneak them into the visiting room. **These are a staple in most South Philly kitchens**—great for breakfast or lunch—so I knew he'd appreciate a taste of home.

1 yellow bell pepper

1 red bell pepper

¼ cup extra-virgin olive oil

Kosher salt and freshly ground black pepper to taste

8 eggs

2 tablespoons chopped fresh Italian parsley

¼ cup grated Parmigiano Reggiano

4 Italian hoagie rolls

Slice each pepper in half, and remove the stems and seeds. Cut the peppers into ¼-inch slices. In a medium pan, heat the olive oil until hot. Add the sliced peppers, season with salt and black pepper, and sauté until tender. Meanwhile, crack the eggs into a separate bowl and beat them together by hand until the whites and yolks are mixed. When the peppers are tender, add the eggs, and scramble them together. Next, heat your oven to 350 degrees F, and slice the rolls three-quarters of the way through, lengthwise. Toast the rolls for 5 minutes, and place the egg-and-pepper mixture inside.

BEEF CARPACCIO

SERVES 4

You can blow your guests away by serving this as a simple appetizer or first course, but for this dish to be really great, **your tenderloin slices need to be superthin.** Here's a trick: **freeze the meat for about an hour ahead of time,** and then use a really sharp knife to slice it. Or have your butcher do it—that's what he's there for. I use a little coarse sea salt to finish the dish; I like the little crunch that the salt provides.

8 ounces beef tenderloin, thinly sliced and pounded

Pinch of flake salt

Pinch of freshly ground black pepper

Carpaccio Sauce (recipe follows)

4 ounces arugula

¼ cup extra-virgin olive oil

Kosher salt to taste, for arugula

1 lemon, for squeezing

6 ounces Parmigiano Reggiano, thinly sliced

Place the pounded beef on a cold plate in one layer, and season with flake salt and pepper. Lightly spread the sauce on top of the beef. In a small bowl, toss the arugula with the olive oil, kosher salt, and a squeeze of lemon. Place the arugula mixture on top of beef. Garnish with slices of grated Parmigiano Reggiano on the beef.

CARPACCIO SAUCE

MAKES 1½ CUPS

1 egg

2 tablespoons freshly squeezed lemon juice

1 cup second-press olive oil

1 teaspoon kosher salt

2 teaspoons Worcestershire sauce

In a medium bowl, blend the egg with 1 tablespoon of the lemon juice. Whisk vigorously while slowly adding in the olive oil until it emulsifies. (It should look like a mayo.) Then add the salt, Worcestershire sauce, and remaining lemon juice, and whisk until combined.

FRIED GALAMAD RED

SERVES 4

You might call it calamari, but we call it galamad in South Philly. Either way—crispy, hot, and sweet—it's a great appetizer.

¼ cup extra-virgin olive oil

4 fresh garlic cloves, smashed

1 red bell pepper

1 yellow bell pepper

1 Italian long hot

20 ounces San Marzano whole tomatoes, hand crushed

Kosher salt and freshly ground pepper to taste

3 fresh basil leaves, torn

1 pound fresh galamad, tubes only, size 5–8

½ cup all-purpose flour

½ cup semolina flour

Granulated garlic to taste

Vegetable oil, for frying

1 tablespoon balsamic reduction (see page 13), plus 1 tablespoon for garnish

In a medium sauté pan, heat the olive oil and add the garlic; cook until golden brown. Next cut the peppers lengthwise, take out all the seeds and stems, and cut each half into quarters. Cut the Italian long hot on the bias into ½-inch pieces. Add the peppers and long hot to the pan, and sauté until they are soft. Next add the San Marzano tomatoes, and season with salt and black pepper. Cover, and simmer for 5 minutes; add the fresh basil, and mix it in.

Cut the galamad into ½-inch pieces. Mix both flours together in a bowl. Put the galamad in a separate bowl, and season with salt, black pepper, and granulated garlic; mix until well blended. Scoop the galamad in flour until it is coated on all sides, and shake off the excess flour before deep-frying. In a deep fryer or deep skillet, heat the vegetable oil to 375 degrees F. (Use a candy thermometer to gauge the correct temperature.) Add the galamad and cook for 4 minutes; cook in batches if necessary to be sure the galamad is not crowded in the deep fryer or pan. When the galamad is tender, add to the sauce and toss. Add the balsamic reduction, and toss together. Place galamad on a serving plate and garnish by drizzling with reduced balsamic.

GRILLED OCTOPUS

SERVES 4 TO 6

When you boil the octopus, toss a wine cork (or two) into the pot. There's something about the cork that makes the octopus tender. Maybe it's a myth, but my octopus has always turned out great.

1 pound Spanish or Portuguese octopus

1 whole lemon, juiced

2 wine corks

⅓ cup red-wine vinegar

½ cup olive oil

1 stalk celery, cut on a bias into ¼-inch pieces

10 black olives, pitted

1 teaspoon kosher salt

1 teaspoon freshly ground black pepper

1 teaspoon granulated garlic

¼ cup finely chopped fresh Italian parsley

1 lemon, cut into wedges

Preheat your grill to 350 degrees F, then boil a large pot of water. Add the octopus, lemon juice, corks, and vinegar, and boil for 25 minutes over medium heat. Check the doneness by inserting a fork into the thickest part of the octopus; if you get no resistance (the fork goes into the meat easily), the octopus is cooked. Remove the octopus from the water with a pair of tongs, and let it cool down on a plate until it's cool to the touch. With a sharp knife, cut the tentacles off, and discard the rest of the octopus.

Place the octopus in a large bowl and coat lightly with 2 tablespoons of the olive oil. Allow the oil to drip off the octopus slightly, then place octopus on the hot grill. If it starts to flame up, you had too much oil on your octopus; remove it from grill, wipe off, and replace. Cook for 3 minutes on each side, making sure to rotate to get the grill marks on the meat.

While the octopus is grilling, toss the remaining olive oil, the celery, olives, salt, pepper, granulated garlic, and parsley in a medium-sized bowl. When the octopus is cooked, cut into ¼-inch cubes. Toss lightly with the vegetables, and divide evenly among your plates. Garnish each plate with a lemon wedge.

FRESH MOZZARELLA

MAKES 8 BALLS

Making your own mozzarella is so simple, but no one ever does it. (You can find the curd in many specialty stores, or online.) **I promise, if you make it yourself, it'll change your fucking life.** I taught Jimmy Kimmel how to make this on his TV show. He went nuts for the stuff.

8 cups water

28 ounces mozzarella curd

8 teaspoons salt

2 tablespoons extra-virgin olive oil
(optional garnish)

Place a stockpot full of water on the stove, and heat to 180 degrees F. (Use a candy thermometer to gauge the correct temperature.) Cut the mozzarella curd into ⅛-inch pieces and put them in a medium bowl—it is important to cut the curd into equal-sized pieces, to ensure they melt evenly. Add the salt to the curd, and pour the water into the bowl, just enough to cover the curd. With a large kitchen spoon, slowly mix the curd. As you mix, the curd will become soft and the lumps will smooth. As the curd comes together, repeatedly fold it over itself until it becomes a single, soft, shiny ball. Pinch off an approximately 5-ounce piece with your hand. Use both hands to stretch the mozzarella and fold it over itself repeatedly until it forms a small ball.

You can serve it warm like this and top with extra-virgin olive oil, or place the mozzarella ball in a bowl of room-temperature water to cool. Repeat this process until all the mozzarella is rolled. For longer storage, wrap each ball in plastic wrap and refrigerate. The balls will keep for up to 2 days.

FRIED MOZZARELLA

SERVES 4

You can find mozzarella sticks at just about any restaurant, but they're usually bland and boring. The difference between mine and theirs? Night and day. I'm the only one I know who uses **fresh mozzarella.** Make it yourself (see preceding recipe), or buy it in the supermarket, but **definitely use it in this recipe.** It will blow your mind.

1 pound fresh mozzarella

2 teaspoons kosher salt

½ teaspoon freshly ground black pepper

2 teaspoons granulated garlic

½ cup all-purpose flour

1 cup vegetable oil

EGG WASH

3 eggs

½ teaspoon kosher salt

½ teaspoon freshly ground black pepper

¼ cup finely chopped fresh Italian parsley

¼ cup grated Parmigiano Reggiano

BREAD-CRUMB MIXTURE

2 cups unseasoned bread crumbs

¼ cup finely chopped fresh Italian parsley

¼ cup grated Parmigiano Reggiano

WHITE SAUCE

¼ cup extra-virgin olive oil

4 garlic cloves, smashed and chopped

1 anchovy fillet, whole

¾ cup chicken stock

2 tablespoons salted butter

2 tablespoons all-purpose flour

TO MAKE THE EGG WASH Crack the eggs into a medium bowl, and add the salt, pepper, parsley, and Parmigiano Reggiano. Whisk together until well blended. In a separate bowl, mix the bread crumbs, parsley, and Parmigiano Reggiano until well combined. Cut the mozzarella into four even slices lengthwise, and season with the salt, pepper, and granulated garlic. Finally, dredge the slices in the flour, then in the egg mixture, and then in the bread-crumb mixture, until all are fully covered with breading. In a medium sauté pan, heat the vegetable oil to 375 degrees F. (Use a candy thermometer to gauge the correct temperature.) Place the breaded mozzarella in the pan, one piece at a time, and fry until it is golden brown on both sides.

TO MAKE THE SAUCE heat the olive oil in a small sauté pan, add the garlic, and cook until almost brown. Then add the anchovy and cook for 2 minutes. Ladle in the chicken stock. Dredge the butter in the flour, and place in pan. Mix until sauce becomes thick enough to coat a spoon.

Divide the mozzarella among four plates, and serve with the sauce on the side or drizzled on top.

MORTADELLA SPREAD

SERVES 4 TO 6

This is my take on chicken-liver pâté. It's the product of just messing around in the kitchen and trying to do something different. Honestly, I've never been a big fan of mortadella, but I wanted to see what else I could do with it—to elevate it. I guess I got it right: I did this appetizer at the James Beard House, and people there flipped over it. Unlike regular ricotta, impastata is whipped and has the consistency of butter. It's got a great, subtle flavor—just a little sweet—that's perfect for this spread. You can find it in Italian specialty stores.

8 ounces mortadella

1 cup heavy cream

4 ounces ricotta impastata

3 ounces Parmigiano Reggiano, grated

Dice the mortadella into ¼-inch pieces, and purée in a food processor. Slowly add the heavy cream, continuing to purée until well blended; be sure to scrape down the sides during this process. Now add the ricotta and Parmigiano Reggiano, and purée once more until well blended.

POTATO AND EGGS

SERVES 4

This embodies the simple pleasures of peasant comfort food—a dish we'd have on Fridays when we couldn't eat meat. *Frittata* wasn't in our vocabulary. Add some grated Parmigiano Reggiano and put this on some crusty bread. **It's stupid-good, cuz.**

¼ cup extra-virgin olive oil

2 Idaho potatoes, peeled and cut into ¼-inch pieces

6 eggs

¼ teaspoon kosher salt

¼ teaspoon freshly ground black pepper

4 Italian hoagie rolls

Heat the olive oil in a medium sauté pan to 350 degrees F. (Use a candy thermometer to gauge the correct temperature.) Fry the potatoes for 5 to 8 minutes, or until golden brown. Meanwhile, crack the eggs into a bowl, and whisk them together. Season with the salt and pepper. Add the eggs to the pan with the potatoes, and scramble them together. Slice the hoagie rolls lengthwise, and place the egg-and-potato mixture inside.

MARTORANO MEATBALLS

MAKES EIGHTEEN 1-INCH MEATBALLS

People call me the **Meatball Mogul.** At one point, I was kind of ashamed of that, because I felt we did a lot of things really well—not just meatballs. When I was in Vegas, I'd run into people on the street, and if they recognized me, they'd say, "You're that meatball guy." Over the years, it's something that I've embraced, and today I actually love it. I realized that you shouldn't run from who you are. Plus, it didn't hurt that *Gourmet* magazine once wrote that I made **the best meatballs in the world.**

½ cup finely chopped fresh Italian parsley

1 pound stale hoagie rolls

½ pound ground beef

½ pound ground veal

½ pound ground pork

2 teaspoons kosher salt

2 teaspoons freshly ground black pepper

2 teaspoons granulated garlic

1 extra-large egg

½ cup grated Parmigiano Reggiano

½ cup unseasoned bread crumbs

3 cups vegetable oil

Finely chop the parsley, allow it to dry for 30 minutes in the open air, and set it aside. Slice your bread into ½-inch pieces, add water, and mash with your hands until it's smooth and the water is incorporated, 6 or 7 minutes. The bread should have a firm but doughy texture. Add your beef, veal, pork, salt, pepper, and granulated garlic to the bread; knead well until all ingredients are thoroughly mixed. Add the egg, the Parmigiano Reggiano, and parsley, kneading again until all ingredients are well combined. Finally, add your bread crumbs and knead well again. Resist the temptation just to throw all the ingredients into a bowl and mix at the same time: the order of procedure in this recipe is very important to the final product.

Divide and weigh the mixture into balls of 5½ ounces, then roll them, using a circular motion between both hands, until your meatballs are round and firm. You will get roughly eighteen balls.

In a 14-inch frying pan, heat the vegetable oil to 325 degrees F. (Use a candy thermometer to gauge the correct temperature.) Once the oil is hot, gently place the meatballs in the oil and cook in batches. The oil should have a slow bubble to it. When the meatballs are light brown in color, flip them over with a pair of tongs, and cook until brown on the other side. The internal temperature of the meatballs should be 150 degrees F.

You can eat the meatballs like this, or add them to the Sunday Pork Gravy recipe (page 78), and let them simmer for 30 minutes before serving. To go over the top, serve with the Martorano Salad (page 15).

MUSSELS MARINARA

SERVES 4

When I first started cooking, I was working in the kitchen at a bar my dad ran called Anton's. The mussels we used were inexpensive, so they needed a pretty serious cleaning. Believe it or not, **I used one of those old-fashioned washing machines, which they had in the basement, to get all the sand out of the mussels.** Today, I buy mussels that are of a much higher quality than what we had in the bar—and don't have to worry about sand or grit. They're pretty clean and easy to work with. You just need to rinse them off and remove the beard.

1 pound mussels

¼ cup extra-virgin olive oil

8 garlic cloves, smashed

12 ounces San Marzano whole
    tomatoes, hand crushed

½ teaspoon kosher salt

¼ teaspoon freshly ground black
    pepper

½ teaspoon granulated garlic

4 fresh basil leaves

¼ teaspoon dried oregano

¼ teaspoon crushed red-pepper
    flakes

Rinse the mussels, and remove the beards.

In a large sauté pan, heat the olive oil and brown the smashed garlic. Then add the San Marzano tomatoes, and season with the salt, black pepper, granulated garlic, basil, oregano, and red-pepper flakes, and add the mussels. Cover, and cook for 8 to 10 minutes. If there are any unopened mussels, discard them. Garnish with toasted bread crumbs.

HOMEMADE TOASTED BREAD CRUMBS

½ cup extra virgin olive oil

1½ cups unseasoned bread crumbs

1 anchovy fillet

4 cloves garlic

2 tablespoons chopped Italian parsley

2 tablespoons Parmigiano Reggiano

Kosher salt and black pepper to taste

In a medium sauté pan over medium heat, add the olive oil and garlic and sauté until brown. Add the anchovy and mix into the oil. Next add in the bread crumbs, and frequently stir to brown evenly, about 5 minutes. Once the bread crumbs have become a caramel-like color, remove from the heat and place in a bowl; allow to cool for 15 minutes. Finally, add the parsley, Parmigiano Reggiano, and salt and pepper.

RICE BALLS

SERVES 4

Aside from Rice-A-Roni, I'm not really a rice guy, and this wasn't something that people in my family made. The first time I ever had a rice ball was in Brooklyn, at a little Italian deli, and I was, like, **"Wow, I get it."** The thing I love about rice balls is that they're a great way to use leftovers—**you can stuff them with whatever you have on hand in the fridge,** which appeals to my style of cooking. You can find the caciocavallo, a gourd-shaped cheese, in Italian specialty stores.

1 envelope of saffron threads (usually .1 gram)

1 cup Pinot Grigio

7 tablespoons salted butter

2 tablespoons finely chopped fresh thyme

1 garlic clove, minced

1 onion, diced

3 cups chicken stock

1 cup Arborio rice

½ cup grated Parmigiano Reggiano

3 ounces caciocavallo

Vegetable oil, for frying

EGG WASH

3 eggs

½ teaspoon kosher salt

½ teaspoon freshly ground black pepper

¼ cup finely chopped fresh Italian parsley

¼ cup grated Parmigiano Reggiano

BREAD-CRUMB MIXTURE

2 cups unseasoned bread crumbs

¼ cup finely chopped fresh Italian parsley

¼ cup grated Parmigiano Reggiano

All-purpose flour, for dredging

Pour the wine into a cup with the saffron, and allow the saffron to bloom. In a large sauté pan, melt the butter, and add the thyme, garlic, and onion, cooking gently until the onion becomes translucent, not brown. In a medium pot, bring the chicken stock to a simmer. When the onion is soft, add the rice, stirring constantly as you cook for 1 minute. Now add the wine to the sauté pan, and allow the rice to absorb it all. Next ladle in the chicken stock, ¾ cup at a time, allowing it to be absorbed into the rice; repeat this process until all of the stock is absorbed into the rice. When it is, remove the risotto from the heat and stir in the Parmigiano Reggiano.

Spread the rice on a sheet pan, and allow it to cool. To make a ball, roll about 2 ounces of rice in your hand; make a hole with your thumb, and place in the caciocavallo inside. Continue rolling until the rice surrounds the cheese. Repeat until all the rice is used.

TO MAKE THE EGG WASH crack the eggs into a medium bowl, and add the salt, pepper, parsley, and Parmigiano Reggiano; whisk until the ingredients are well blended.

In a separate bowl, add the bread crumbs, parsley, and Parmigiano Reggiano. Mix until well combined, and set aside. Dredge the rice balls in the flour, shaking off the excess. Dip each rice ball into the egg wash, and then coat with the bread-crumb mixture. Repeat until all the rice balls are breaded, making sure each is fully coated.

Preheat your deep fryer to 350 degrees F (use a candy thermometer to gauge the temperature), and fry the rice balls a few at a time for 3 to 4 minutes, or until they are golden brown. Serve hot.

STUFFED HOT PEPPERS

SERVES 4 TO 6

Finding a fresh Italian long hot outside of Philly or the Northeast might be a little tough. **Anaheim peppers are a perfect substitute** and will be easier to find.

⅓ cup extra-virgin olive oil, plus more for garnish

18 ounces ground veal

⅓ cup whole garlic cloves, smashed and roughly chopped

½ white onion

4 sprigs fresh sage, chopped

2 ounces Parmigiano Reggiano

8 ounces Fresh Mozzarella (page 29), cubed, plus 2 ounces grated

1 tablespoon finely chopped fresh Italian parsley

2 tablespoons unseasoned bread crumbs

1 teaspoon kosher salt

1 teaspoon granulated garlic

½ teaspoon freshly ground black pepper

Vegetable oil, for frying

8 Italian long hots

Pinch of crushed red-pepper flakes

Heat a medium sauté pan, add the olive oil and ground veal, and cook until brown. Add garlic, and cook until brown. Add the onion and sage, mixing well, and cook until tender. Cool in a separate bowl, and set aside. To the same sauté pan, add the Parmigiano Reggiano, cubed mozzarella, parsley, bread crumbs, and seasonings. Take the Italian long hot peppers and blanch-fry in a deep fryer at 325 degrees F for 1 minute. When they're cool, slice the peppers lengthwise, remove the seeds, and stuff the veal mixture into them. Place the peppers in a pan with olive oil on the bottom, so they don't stick. Cook for 5 minutes over medium heat, or until the peppers are hot; then top with grated fresh mozzarella cheese and allow it to melt. Serve on individual plates, and garnish with olive oil and red-pepper flakes.

THE GINK'S WILD MUSHROOM SAUTÉ

SERVES 4

My grandfather on my father's side was named George Martorano, but my grandmother called him "The Gink." He was born in Sicily and was a great cook. **He would get up early every day and go food shopping for fresh ingredients.** When he went wild-mushroom hunting, he brought me and my father along. Some wild mushrooms are poisonous so my grandmother would make my grandfather eat them first before she gave any to the kids. You don't need wild mushrooms for this appetizer (which goes great on crusty Italian bread). A mix of oyster, portobello, shiitake, and button mushrooms will get you the same result.

2 garlic cloves

¼ cup extra-virgin olive oil, plus 2 tablespoons for the 8 mushrooms

1 anchovy fillet, whole

½ cup unseasoned bread crumbs

1 tablespoon grated Parmigiano Reggiano

1 tablespoon finely chopped fresh Italian parsley

Granulated garlic to taste

Kosher salt and freshly ground black pepper to taste

8 ounces mushrooms (any kinds; see headnote), roughly chopped

1 loaf crusty Italian bread, sliced

On a clean cutting board, mince the garlic; set aside. In a medium sauté pan, heat 2 tablespoons of the olive oil; add half of the garlic. When the garlic becomes slightly brown, add the anchovy, and continue to cook until the garlic is brown. Add the bread crumbs, and reduce the heat to medium; toast, stirring occasionally with a spoon so the crumbs don't burn, until they become evenly golden brown. Remove from the heat, and add the Parmigiano Reggiano and chopped parsley, mixing them well into the bread crumbs. Remove from the pan and set aside.

To make the mushrooms, heat a medium sauté pan and slowly add the remaining olive oil and garlic; sauté until golden brown. Then add the mushrooms and season with granulated garlic, salt, and pepper. Sauté for 8 to 10 minutes over medium heat. Cook until the mushrooms become soft, and then finish with the parsley-and-bread-crumb mixture. This side dish should look and feel dry, not wet. Serve on slices of crusty Italian bread.

LEFT *The Gink*

WINGS BIBZ STYLE

SERVES 6 TO 8

"Bibz" was my nickname when I was a kid—I feel like my mom kept me in a bib until I was thirty-two years old—so this sauce is named for me. I love two kinds of food: Italian (obviously) and Chinese. I got the idea for this recipe when I was fooling around in the kitchen, trying to bring these two loves together. What I came up with was something sweet, sour, and spicy. I don't care if it's Chinese or Italian—if it has a lot of flavor, we'll put it on the menu.

¼ cup extra-virgin olive oil

½ cup whole garlic cloves, finely chopped

3 cups chicken stock

1½ cups sweet chili sauce

2 tablespoons hoisin sauce

1 tablespoon butter

1 tablespoon all-purpose flour

Vegetable oil, for frying

36 first-and-second-joint chicken wings

¼ cup toasted sesame seeds

TO MAKE THE SAUCE Heat the olive oil in a small pot, and cook the chopped garlic until brown. Add the chicken stock, sweet chili sauce, and hoisin sauce. Bring the sauce to a boil, then lower to a simmer and reduce the sauce by half. Dredge the butter in flour, add it to the pan, and allow it to melt into the sauce thickening it.

Preheat a deep fryer to 350 degrees F. When the oil is hot, place dry wings in the basket and lower them slowly. Cook the wings until fully done and at an internal temperature of 165 degrees F, about 12 minutes. Set aside, then toss with Bibz sauce and sesame seeds.

YO CUZ!

BEGINNINGS

I LEARNED TWO THINGS from my paternal grandmother: how to cook and how to curse. It seemed like every other word out of her mouth was *fuck.* (When I was a little boy, she watched me while my mom worked, so I picked up the habit naturally, I guess. It's just what she said, the way she talked: "Go get me a pack of fucking cigarettes." "Go get me a fucking beach chair." "Go put the fucking pot of water on." Everyone gathered at her house on Sundays—neighbors, family, and their kids—and there was always a feast, a *fucking* feast.

Gram (her name was Mary) was old-school Italian. She and my grandfather came from *It-lee* (Italy), and had a pretty big family: four sons—Raymond, Joe, John, and Anthony—and two daughters— Angie and Phyllis. Gram never worked, but she always had money; nobody ever understood how or why. She kept it hidden in her bra. You needed money? You'd go to Gram and she'd reach into her bra and peel out the cash—$5, $10, $20. Then she'd whisper, "Don't fucking tell nobody."

> You needed money? You'd go to Gram and she'd reach into her bra and peel out the cash—$5, $10, $20. Then she'd whisper, "Don't fucking tell nobody."

Gram made homemade ravioli, spaghetti, and the best ricotta gnocchi. We usually ate Sunday dinner at 5:00 p.m., but by eight o'clock Gram would call me into the kitchen and bring out two jars of pickled pigs' feet that my grandfather had made. I'd climb into her lap, and Gram would feed me pickled pigs' feet; we'd put ketchup on them. Her love and her food kept our family together.

My paternal grandfather was named George Martorano. He might have cooked even more than my grandmother. His specialty was sautéed wild mushrooms.

My maternal grandfather, Anthony Durante, died before I was born. They said he was a tough son of a bitch; his nickname was "The Wolf."

I remember my mother telling me that my grandfather shot somebody in the neighborhood because this guy took a piss in front of my mother and family as they were taking a walk. My grandfather got furious, took everyone home, got his gun, and left the house. He didn't come back for a week. In the meantime, my grandmother heard that a guy had been shot the night my grandfather disappeared, and she figured my grandfather was hiding out until things cooled down. As a kid, I remember seeing an old man limping in my neighborhood; I always imagined that was the guy my grandfather shot.

Sue Durante, whom I called Nanny, was my maternal grandmother and lived with us. Nanny was widowed at an early age, left to raise my mom and her two brothers, Tony and Louie. Compared with Gram, Nanny was more of a modern grandmother. She worked, shopped, and loved to play bingo. On the side, she took numbers on Saturdays. Neighbors and friends—maybe twenty or thirty people—would call the house with their bets on a number. A quarter bet could score you $100. It was a good way to make a little extra cash in the neighborhood. But eventually the government figured that out, made it illegal, and started their own lotteries.

My mother, like hers, was a modern woman for her time, and worked in a place that manufactured bathing suits. Lillian Martorano was beautiful—fairly tall for an Italian woman (five foot seven or so) with reddish-blond hair, and always sharp-looking and well dressed. People wanted to know who she was whenever she walked into a room—she was that kind of woman. Because my grandfather Durante died when she was young, my mother worked pretty much all of her life and, until she got married and had a family of her own, she gave her paycheck

Compared with Gram, Nanny was more of a modern grandmother. She worked, shopped, and loved to play bingo. On the side, she took numbers on Saturdays.

ABOVE *Uncle Anthony Durante, "The Wolf"*

to Nanny. But even though she worked a lot, my mother could cook one helluva meal.

We didn't have a whole lot of money, so some of her best dishes were her most basic. One of my favorites was pastina with butter, a dish I serve to this day. In the wintertime, when it was really cold, we'd watch our favorite TV shows, *The Honeymooners* and *Sanford and Son,* and eat what we called "Italian soul food." My mother took that great American standby, the hot dog, cut it up, and served it along with bell peppers. Hot dogs and peppers was peasant food, but we felt we were feasting on filet mignon.

My father, Joe Martorano, was a heavy guy—five foot ten, about 250 pounds. He did whatever he had to do to make a buck, keep a roof over our heads, and put food on the table. He wasn't a fancy guy—didn't care for cars, clothes, or a big house—but he was loyal as hell and respected by everyone. He taught me that relationships are very important in life. As long as things were good with his family, he was a very happy guy who loved to joke around. He also did some loan-sharking. When I bought my first car, I borrowed the money from him. I had to pay it all back, plus the interest, just to teach me responsibility. Even though his main job was driving a truck for the vending company, when I was a little older he ran a bar/restaurant in South Philly called Anton's, at 11th and Ellsworth, and it was there that I got my first true professional cooking experience.

Both businesses were owned by his brother Raymond—a man who had a ton of influence not just over my father but over our entire family.

TO ME, HE WAS JUST UNCLE RAYMOND, but in the newspaper headlines it was always Raymond "Long John" Martorano.

Legend had it, he got the nickname when he was a kid because he always wore long underwear under his clothes.

Of course, my cousins and I didn't have the balls to call him "Long John"—at least not to his face—and in return he never called us by our names. It was always, "Howya doin', kid?" or "How's my nephew?" That kind of shit made me nervous, but as a kid you weren't going to get much more out of him. When Uncle Raymond was around, we were on our best behavior.

ABOVE *My dad, Joe Martorano*

More often than not, though, it seemed Uncle Raymond wasn't around. When he went away to prison, we only saw him if he requested to see us. My cousins or I would smuggle pepper-and-egg and chicken-cutlet sandwiches into the joint, stuffing the food in our socks and down our pants so we wouldn't get caught—if you got caught, they took the food and you lost your visiting privileges. He'd always ask about our families, and then take us aside individually for one-to-one talks.

My cousins or I would smuggle pepper-and-egg and chicken-cutlet sandwiches into the joint, stuffing the food in our socks and down our pants so we wouldn't get caught.

Once, when I was visiting my uncle Raymond in prison, he told me the story of "The Scorpion and the Turtle": A scorpion and a turtle lived near a river. One day the river was rising and threatened to flood the riverbank and kill the scorpion, who couldn't swim. The scorpion asked the turtle for a favor. "Please," he said, "let me hop on the back of your shell, and take me to the other side of the river." The turtle said no, fearing the scorpion would bite and kill him. "I give you my word," said the scorpion, "I won't bite you." The turtle agreed, and the pair made their way to the other side of the river. However, when they made land, the scorpion bit the turtle. Shocked and disappointed, the turtle asked why the scorpion had gone back on his word. "I am what I am," said the scorpion.

I loved that story because it taught me to look out for myself, that there are people who have it in their nature to take advantage of you. Scorpion? Turtle? I didn't want to be either one, but in South Philly there weren't a lot of other options. Plus, whatever I did, I wanted my family to be as proud of me as they were of Uncle Raymond. Yeah, I know he was in prison, but it didn't matter to us—in South Philly, the man was considered a success.

When he got out of prison, Uncle Raymond was always busy on the streets, turning the Martorano name into something honorable, something that demanded respect. In our neighborhood, if you needed something, you went to him. Couldn't pay the electric bill? Go see Raymond. Young guys in the neighborhood getting too big for their balls? Raymond. Trouble with the boss at work? You guessed it. Uncle Raymond knew everyone, and everyone knew him. He was respected, but also feared. These two things were kind of interchangeable in my neighborhood.

On one of my aunt's birthdays, the year I turned seventeen, Uncle

Raymond took our family to the Latin Casino, across the river, in Cherry Hill, New Jersey, to see Frank Sinatra perform. What a treat! I was raised on Sinatra; in 1998, when he died, I even got a tattoo of Ol' Blue Eyes. As a kid, I learned all his songs by listening to a couple of local radio shows called *Friday with Frank* and *Sunday with Sinatra,* hosted by a DJ named Sid Mark. At the time,

Meatballs and Sinatra at home was a religious experience

everyone had long hair and was listening to The Who and The Rolling Stones, but I remained a die-hard Sinatra man. On Sundays, my buddies would come over and we'd drive down to this lake in Philadelphia, where we washed and waxed our cars. We wore white wifebeater T-shirts and black slacks and kept our hair nice and short. And as we cleaned our cars and cruised for girls, we'd blast *Sunday with Sinatra* from the car radios. Then we'd come home, and my mother would leave out a bowl of fried meatballs for us. We made fried-meatball sandwiches and listened to Sinatra.

Meatballs and Sinatra at home was a religious experience already, but to see him in person with Uncle Raymond took things to a whole new level. When the Chairman of the Board walked onstage that night at the Latin Casino, he walked over to our front-row table, greeted the entire Martorano family, and then extended his hand to my aunt. As an Italian-American, I felt like we were getting a blessing from Jesus Christ. And being around Uncle Raymond was like spending time with the pope.

And you don't fuck with the pope.

I WAS THE SON of a guy who worked in the vending-machine business, so my pockets didn't bulge with wads of cash like Raymond's—they jingled. My allowance and school tuition were paid in change: quarters, dimes, and nickels. I admired my parents for working hard, but having real money— a roll of bills—was all that mattered to me. Money was power to me.

Despite my parents' financial circumstances, they never complained— especially my father, who never seemed to get a break in life. Even though the vending business was a family operation, he usually got the short end of the stick. His brothers Raymond and John ran the business side, while my father and his other brother, Anthony, did the labor part of the work.

ABOVE *Raymond "Long John" Martorano*

"Joe, deliver these cigarettes." "Deliver this jukebox." Do this and do that–that kind of shit. But back then family members helped each other, they were loyal, and even if they didn't like something, they kept their mouths shut.

When gambling was legalized in Atlantic City, my father began renting a van and charging guys for a ride to the Resorts Casino. Since he wasn't a gambler or a drinker, while his crew spent all their money in the casino and got drunk, my father would walk around or stand with his hands behind his back, waiting for them. Then, after the guys had lost all their money, my dad would loan them more–a couple of hundred bucks here and there. Eventually, instead of waiting around for hours, he started selling nylons to the cocktail waitresses out of his van. Three pairs for a dollar, four for a dollar–whatever he had to do to make a buck, that's what my father did. I respected him for that.

Everything he got was a hand-me-down from his brothers. Once, he drove home a white Cadillac. His big new car was really Uncle John's old one, but my father didn't care. It was new to him and new to us. In the mid-1970s, when I was in high school, my father had an opportunity to be head of the Bartenders Union in Atlantic City–a dream job arranged by Uncle Raymond. But before he even started, Angelo Bruno and Uncle Raymond took it away: it wouldn't look good to the feds, they decided, if there were too many Martoranos running things. My father never said a word, showing only love and respect. In private, I could tell he and my mother were hurt, but I knew it was only business.

MY PARENTS always stressed the importance of a good education, but I was never cut out for school. The nuns at King of Peace Elementary, at 26th and Wharton, didn't show much interest in me, probably because I didn't show much interest in learning. All my friends had nicknames like "Weasel," "Fish," and "Petey Pump." As I told you, mine was "Stevie Truck." I guess everyone figured I'd be doing the same as my dad one day.

In the sixth grade, I stopped giving a shit about school once and for all, thanks to a particularly miserable nun. Once, she sent me home with all F's on my report card. On the way home that Friday–with the whole weekend in front of me–I decided to take a pen and turn the F's into B's. Unfortunately, my parents didn't buy it. They let it slide for almost the entire weekend before confronting me, but by that point, my father was furious. "All the money I spend sending you to private school and this is what I get?" he said. "Enough of the bullshit."

Eventually, school even ruined lunch, my favorite part of the day. From first to fifth grade, we could bring our own from home, but beginning in the sixth grade, we had to buy it from the school cafeteria. Sloppy Joes? Canned tomato soup? I wouldn't have any part of it. Instead, my mother would make me a potato-and-egg sandwich, or a chicken cutlet with lettuce, tomato, and mayo. I'd sneak the sandwich into my book bag and stash it in my locker. Then, at lunchtime, I stopped by my locker and grabbed my lunch, went into the bathroom, locked the door, sat on the toilet, and ate my sandwich. I prayed no one had to take a shit.

> **Eventually, school even ruined lunch, my favorite part of the day.**

I guess I was in grade school when I opened my first takeout business. I'd have my mother pack me a few extra sandwiches every day, then eat one and sell the others. Business was booming–that is, until my friend Joey started stealing the goods. At first, I couldn't figure out what was happening to the sandwiches. Then, one day, in the middle of class, I looked out the door and saw that fat bastard in the hallway dangling my lunch bag and wiping his mouth. I tried to solve the problem by hiding my lunch in different spots every day. Didn't matter, though–he'd always find it.

By high school, at Bishop Neumann, my grades had gotten a lot better, but not because my study habits had improved. During the gas shortages of the seventies, when people needed vouchers to purchase gasoline, I got them for my teachers, and they all gave me passing grades. I barely had to go to class. Instead, I spent my day in the audiovisual room, thinking of ways to earn more money. I probably bumped into my teachers more at nightclubs than I did in classrooms.

But when I did attend class–or go anywhere, for that matter–I was determined to look sharp, like Uncle Raymond. Dress shirt, tie, shined shoes–people started calling me "Marvelous Martorano." I even started my own number-and-sports betting business to add to the money I made delivering dry-cleaning and painting houses. When I went into Mr. Carapucci's history class, I would put the winning number on the blackboard before the bell rang. Then Carapucci would come into class and erase the number, but he was cool about it.

"Marvelous," he'd say, "that's enough." Then he'd laugh.

If there was a moneymaking scheme, I was in the middle of it. I was determined always to have cash. To me, cash was power. You couldn't buy nice things with nickels and dimes, and having money made me feel like I had more power.

EVEN THOUGH my father only made $166 a week at the vending company (up until the day he died), he always sent my mother, Nanny, and me to the Jersey Shore for two weeks each summer—no matter what. My father would come on Saturday night and leave Sunday morning to go back to work. His real vacation, though, was one week out of the year, to go hunting in the Pocono Mountains. But I never really got into hunting. I loved the sun and water much more, so I taught myself how to surf; I'm sure I was the only kid in South Philly with a surfboard strapped on top of a 1974 Caddy. I guess I just wanted to be different—from my father and everyone else.

Never forget who you are and where you came from.

While we stayed in a motel down the Shore, in Wildwood, New Jersey, Uncle Raymond spent his summer weekends there in his second house, with a pool. He and Uncle Anthony had married sisters from Wildwood— the Pizza girls—whose family owned A & LP, a little grocery store that had the best hoagies around, with mounds of Genoa salami, cappicola, and prosciutto on Italian bread. We'd get the hoagies to go, then head to Uncle Raymond's house, at 17th and New Jersey, for a swim. He'd be out back, cleaning out the pool. It relaxed him.

When I turned eighteen, after high-school graduation, hanging around with my family in Wildwood for a couple of weeks during the summer just didn't cut it any longer. All I wanted to do year-round was hit the beach during the day and then go out to the clubs with my friends at night. I got permission to stay through August, and planned to stay with some South Philly friends who had a house for the summer. My mother took care of me that summer like I'd never left her house. Each weekend she brought food and clean clothes and collected my dirty laundry. My father was tougher on me: he demanded that I get a job.

ABOVE *Uncle Anthony Martorano*

In high school, I had started lifting weights. That made me

a natural to work the door as a bouncer at the Court Room, a nightclub on the Shore. I quickly gained a reputation. I didn't take shit from anybody. I didn't give a fuck who they were, or who they were with. I had a certain way of running that door, and that's the way I ran it. Respect me and the place where I worked, and I'd respect you. That's the way I was raised. Work—legal or illegal—made a man worthy of your admiration.

> **Work—legal or illegal—made a man worthy of your admiration.**

Toward the end of that summer in Wildwood, I made my way up the street to another club, the Mansion, and ran into Bobby Pantano, a well-known disc jockey who worked there. Bobby was aware that I had a passion for music, and he introduced me to his manager, John Ritchie, with the idea that I could become a disc jockey. Ritchie, who associated with wiseguys around the entertainment business, offered to manage me. But first I had to buy equipment.

The cost was close to $3,000. I knew I didn't have the money. Though I left for home disappointed, my mind was still at work.

Immediately, my mother knew something was wrong. I told her the story; she called my father into the kitchen. Asking for $3,000 was like asking my father for a million.

"Jesus Christ. Are you kidding me?" he yelled. "That's a lot of money."

My father left the room, came back into the kitchen, and handed me the money.

"This is a loan," he said.

I bought the equipment, but knew I had to repay the loan, plus the interest—just like his Atlantic City buddies. With no money or real skills and barely an education, I went to the one place I knew I could make money. I headed for the streets. I would stand on the corner of 29th and Snyder, where Uncle Raymond also had a drugstore. There, I decided, I would sell produce—tomatoes, peppers, lettuce. It was a cash business—no rent, no gas, no electric.

I wasn't going to drive a truck or be on the corner for the rest of my life, though. Those damn nuns hadn't taught me much—that was for sure—but I knew I wasn't going to be "Stevie Truck" forever.

YO CUZ!

MACARONI

BUCATINI CARBONARA

SERVES 4

Using quality ingredients is the key to all Italian cooking. For this recipe, you're already using decadent ingredients, like heavy cream (we never had that when I was a kid—too expensive) and pancetta, which is basically Italian bacon. But **don't skimp when it comes to the eggs.** Use the freshest you can find—organic if they're available. You'll notice a difference, and so will your dinner guests. And if you really want to knock everyone on their asses, garnish the dish with the egg yolks tableside.

1 tablespoon butter

7 ounces pancetta

1 quart heavy cream

Kosher salt and freshly cracked black pepper to taste

4 ounces Parmigiano Reggiano, grated

Sea salt, for pasta water

1 pound bucatini

2 egg yolks, plus 2 more for garnish

In a heated medium sauté pan, melt the butter; add the pancetta. Render down the pancetta until it is cooked, 2 or 3 minutes. Then, slowly, add your heavy cream, and allow it to reduce by half. Taste the cream, since the pancetta has a lot of salt, and salt to taste. Next, season with pepper and stir in the Parmigiano Reggiano until incorporated. Set aside.

In a medium stockpot, boil salted water and cook the bucatini until al dente. Strain the pasta through a colander, and pour into a bowl. Immediately add two of the egg yolks to the pasta, tossing well.

Add the pasta to the sauce, and mix until incorporated. Divide the pasta among four plates, and garnish with the remaining egg yolks and freshly cracked black pepper. Serve right away.

DUCK **BOLOGNESE**

SERVES 6

I'm a fan of cooking meat on the bone and tossing it in with macaroni, and an even bigger fan of dark meat. This recipe—one I created for people who come into my restaurants twice a week and are looking for something different—covers both of those bases. Duck has such a unique flavor. It makes a great new spin on a traditional dish.

½ cup vegetable oil

6 duck legs (thigh and drumstick)

Kosher salt and freshly ground black pepper to taste

Granulated garlic to taste

½ cup extra-virgin olive oil

10 fresh garlic cloves

3 carrots, diced

3 stalks celery, diced

1 white onion

One 6-ounce can tomato paste

1 cup Chianti

14.5 ounces chicken stock

One 28-ounce can San Marzano whole tomatoes, hand crushed

3 bay leaves, dried

Sea salt, for pasta water

1 pound pappardelle

3 ounces ricotta salata

Preheat the oven to 375 degrees F. In a large ovenproof pan with an ovenproof lid, heat the vegetable oil over medium heat. Season the duck legs heavily with salt, pepper, and granulated garlic. When the oil is hot but not smoking, carefully place the duck in it, skin side down, and allow the duck to get golden brown on both sides, about 6 minutes on each side. Remove the duck from the pan, and discard the used vegetable oil. Place the pan back over the heat, and add the olive oil; add the whole garlic cloves, and brown. Now add the carrots and celery, and cook for 3 minutes. Then add the onion, and sauté until translucent. Next, add the tomato paste, and mix until all the vegetables are coated. Deglaze the pan with the wine, and let it be absorbed into the vegetables. Add the chicken stock, tomatoes, and bay leaves; taste, and season again with salt, pepper, and granulated garlic.

Return the seared duck to the sauce, making sure all of the meat is covered with sauce. Cover the pot, and cook in the preheated oven for 3 hours. Check for doneness by picking up the duck legs; the meat should start to pull away from the bone. At this time, with a pair of tongs, carefully take the legs out of the sauce and allow them to cool. When the meat is cool to the touch, pull it apart, and discard the bones. Return the pulled meat to the sauce.

Meanwhile, in boiling salted water, cook the pappardelle, for 8 minutes or until al dente; strain the pasta through a colander, and add it to the sauce, tossing so the pasta is coated with the sauce. Using a pair of tongs, evenly divide the pasta among six plates, and top with the remaining sauce. Garnish with freshly grated ricotta salata.

GUANCIALE AND ONIONS AMATRICIANA

SERVES 4

Like pancetta, **guanciale is unsmoked Italian pork.** It's basically jowl bacon, or bacon from a pig's cheek. I like it better than pancetta, because it's a little sweeter and meatier, but you can use either.

½ red onion

¼ cup extra-virgin olive oil

2 ounces guanciale or pancetta

4 fresh garlic cloves, smashed

6 ounces San Marzano whole
  tomatoes, crushed

¼ cup Pinot Grigio

Kosher salt and freshly ground black
  pepper to taste

Crushed red-pepper flakes to taste

Granulated garlic to taste

Sea salt, for pasta water

4 ounces bucatini

2 ounces Pecorino Romano, grated

4 fresh basil leaves, torn

On a clean cutting board, remove the skin from the onion and slice it into ¼-inch juliennes.

Put a medium sauté pan over medium-high heat; add the olive oil and guanciale. Render down the guanciale, about 3 minutes; then add the smashed garlic, and cook until it is golden brown. Add the onion juliennes, and cook until tender. Finally, add the crushed San Marzano tomatoes, and season with salt, black pepper, red-pepper flakes, and granulated garlic.

In a medium stockpot, boil salted water and cook the bucatini until al dente. Strain the macaroni through a colander, and add it and the Pecorino Romano to the sauce, tossing well. Divide the pasta and sauce among four plates, or serve on a platter. Finish the dish with torn fresh basil.

FUSILLI POLLO

SERVES 4

When it comes to Italian food, I'm somewhat of a purist. I'm not the guy who orders fettuccine with grilled chicken on top. We get a lot of customers in our Florida restaurants who are watching their weight, so I created this dish. **Chicken isn't an add-on here—it's the star of the show.**

Four 6-ounce skinless, boneless chicken breasts halves

Kosher salt and freshly ground black pepper to taste

All-purpose flour, for dredging

Granulated garlic to taste

Vegetable oil, for frying

1 red bell pepper

1 yellow bell pepper

8 garlic cloves

¼ cup extra-virgin olive oil

¼ cup Pinot Grigio

1 cup San Marzano whole tomatoes, hand crushed

Sea salt, for pasta water

1 pound fusilli

¼ cup grated Parmigiano Reggiano

10 fresh basil leaves, torn

EGG WASH

3 eggs

½ teaspoon kosher salt

½ teaspoon freshly ground black pepper

¼ cup finely chopped fresh Italian parsley

¼ cup grated Parmigiano Reggiano

BREAD-CRUMB MIXTURE

2 cups unseasoned bread crumbs

¼ cup finely chopped fresh Italian parsley

¼ cup grated Parmigiano Reggiano

TO MAKE THE EGG WASH Crack the eggs into a medium bowl, and add the salt, pepper, parsley, and Parmigiano Reggiano. Whisk together until well blended. In a separate bowl, mix the bread crumbs, parsley, and Parmigiano Reggiano; set aside.

On a clean cutting board, cut the chicken breasts in half lengthwise. On a separate plate, season the chicken on both sides with salt, pepper, and granulated garlic. Dredge them in the flour, shaking off any excess. Dip each breast piece into the egg wash, and then coat in the bread-crumb mixture.

Heat a large sauté pan with vegetable oil, and add the chicken; fry until both sides are golden brown. You do not want to cook the chicken fully now, because you are going to add it into the sauce; if it is fully cooked when you add it to the pan, it might become dry. When the chicken is golden brown, remove it from heat and slice it into ½-inch pieces. Discard the oil.

TO PREPARE THE SAUCE Slice the peppers in half lengthwise, and remove the stems and seeds. Cut the pepper halves into quarters, getting eight pieces out of each pepper, and set aside. Smash the garlic cloves, and set aside. In a medium pan, heat the olive oil, add garlic to the hot oil, and brown. Next add the peppers, and sauté until tender. Add the chicken breast and basil. Remove the pan from the heat (so the wine won't cause a flame) and add Pinot Grigio. Return the pan to the heat and deglaze, cooking until most of the liquid has evaporated. Then add the crushed San Marzano tomatoes, and season with salt, black pepper, and granulated garlic. Cover, reduce the heat to medium-low, and allow the sauce and chicken to cook for 5 to 7 minutes.

Meanwhile, boil salted water and cook the fusilli until al dente. Strain the pasta through a colander, then add it to the pan, and toss the pasta with the sauce. Divide the pasta and sauce among four plates, or serve on a platter. Finish the dish with grated Parmigiano Reggiano and torn fresh basil.

LINGUINE WITH CLAMS

SERVES 4

My entire cooking philosophy changed 30 years ago, after I saw this being made at Umbertos Clam House on Mulberry Street in New York. At the time, I was running a restaurant, but I didn't really know what I was doing. I had no one to teach me. I arrived at Umbertos late in the morning, and there was already a line forming. When I got in, I saw why. Chefs were cooking pasta to order, and using real clams instead of opening a can of Progresso clam sauce. Stop the fucking presses, I thought. This was an epiphany. I went back for a late lunch, and then again for dinner. When I returned to Philly, **I made a vow: I wasn't going to take any more shortcuts,** and I was going to use only the best products available. By the way, save the clam shells after making this dish and use them for Clams Martorano (page 104). Just rinse the shells clean and freeze them.

¼ cup extra-virgin olive oil

6 garlic cloves, smashed

Pinch of crushed red-pepper flakes

2 tablespoons roughly chopped fresh Italian parsley

24 Rhode Island top neck clams, shucked, juices reserved

Sea salt, for pasta water

1 pound linguine

In a medium sauté pan, heat the olive oil, add the smashed garlic, and allow it to brown. Add the red-pepper flakes and parsley, and cook together for 2 minutes. Remove the pan from the heat, and slowly add the juice from the clams. Once the juices start to bubble and foam, return the pan to the heat, add the clams, and cook for 3 to 4 minutes.

In a large pot of boiling salted water, cook the linguine until al dente. Strain the pasta through a colander, and add it to the pan, tossing in the sauce until well combined. Divide the pasta and sauce among four plates, or serve on a platter.

MACARONI AND GALAMAD GRAVY

SERVES 6 TO 8

Timing is really important when cooking the galamad. You can either fry it quickly—90 seconds, max—or stew it for a long time—45 minutes to an hour. Anything in between and it'll be tough.

½ cup extra-virgin olive oil

1 cup whole garlic cloves, smashed

2 pounds fresh galamad, cut into ½-inch pieces

One 6-ounce can tomato paste

One 28-ounce can San Marzano whole tomatoes, hand crushed

6 fresh basil leaves, torn

Kosher salt and freshly ground black pepper to taste

Sea salt, for pasta water

1 pound spaghetti

In a large pot, heat the olive oil; add the garlic, and cook until it is golden brown. Next add the cut-up galamad. When the galamad starts to turn whiter and plump up, add the tomato paste, and mix together. Cook for 2 or 3 minutes; then add the San Marzano tomatoes, cover, and cook for 45 to 60 minutes over medium heat. Finally, add the fresh torn basil and taste for seasoning.

In a separate pot, boil salted water and cook your spaghetti until al dente. Strain the pasta through a colander, and add it to the sauce, tossing until well combined. Divide the pasta and sauce among 6 to 8 plates, or serve on a platter.

LINGUINE AGLIO E OLIO

SERVES 4

I'm a big believer that a sauce can wait for macaroni, but macaroni can never wait for sauce. In a way, macaroni needs to be treated like a piece of meat—you can undercook or overcook it. The water it boils in needs to be salty (some say it needs to "taste of the sea"), and, once it's cooked, the macaroni should be al dente—should bite back a bit when you eat it. Different cuts cook for different amounts of time. Check the package, but also use your head. And don't let the macaroni sit in a pot of water after it's already been cooked, because it will continue to cook. **It needs to go immediately from the water to the sauce to the plate. End of story.**

1 cup extra-virgin olive oil

3 anchovy fillets, whole

Pinch of crushed red-pepper flakes

Pinch of kosher salt

1 bunch fresh Italian parsley, roughly chopped

Sea salt, for pasta water

1 pound linguine

BREAD-CRUMB MIXTURE

2 garlic cloves

¼ cup extra-virgin olive oil

1 anchovy fillet

½ cup bread crumbs

1 tablespoon grated Parmigiano Reggiano

1 tablespoon roughly chopped fresh Italian parsley

TO MAKE THE BREAD-CRUMB MIXTURE On a clean cutting board, mince the garlic, and set aside. In a medium sauté pan over medium-high heat, heat the olive oil, and add half of the garlic. When it becomes slightly brown, add the anchovy, and continue to cook until the garlic is brown. Add the bread crumbs and reduce the heat to medium; stir occasionally with a spoon so they don't burn. Toast the bread-crumb mixture until it becomes evenly golden brown. Remove from the heat, add Parmigiano Reggiano and parsley, mix well, and set aside.

Place a sauté pan over medium-low heat, and add the olive oil and the remaining garlic. Cook the garlic it browns. Add the anchovies, red-pepper flakes, and salt.

In a pot, bring salted water to a boil and cook the linguine until al dente. Strain the pasta through a colander, and reserve the water. Add 2 tablespoons of the pasta water to the sauce. Toss the linguine into the sauce, then divide among four plates. After you've plated the pasta, garnish it with the bread-crumb mixture on top.

PENNE EGGPLANT

SERVES 4

In Sicily, this is known as pasta alla Norma. Who's Norma? Who the hell knows? **The important thing is to buy quality eggplants.** Make sure they're thin ones—these taste better and have fewer seeds. If you can't find Sicilian eggplant, try Japanese.

2 large eggplants (see headnote)

½ teaspoon kosher salt, plus more for fried eggplant

¼ cup extra-virgin olive oil

8 garlic cloves, smashed

12 ounces San Marzano whole tomatoes, hand crushed

¼ teaspoon freshly ground black pepper

½ teaspoon granulated garlic

4 fresh basil leaves, torn

5 ounces fresh mozzarella, cut into ¼-inch pieces

Sea salt, for pasta water

12 ounces penne

Peel the eggplants until all of the skin is removed, and cut into ½-inch pieces. Preheat your deep fryer to 350 degrees F. (Use a candy thermometer to gauge the correct temperature.) Fry the eggplants until the pieces turn brown. Remove them, and place on a paper towel on a plate. Season the eggplant with a pinch of salt. In a sauté pan, heat the olive oil and brown the smashed garlic. Then add the San Marzano tomatoes, and season with the salt, pepper, and granulated garlic. Cook for 4 minutes, and then add the freshly torn basil, cooked eggplant, and mozzarella.

In a large pot, boil salted water and cook the macaroni until al dente. Drain the pasta in a colander, then add it to the sauce, tossing and coating the macaroni. Divide the pasta and sauce among four plates, or serve on a platter.

ORECCHIETTE WITH BROCCOLI RABE

SERVES 4

This dish originates from the Puglia region of Italy. The main ingredient is rapini, or broccoli rabe. It's bitter. Some people adore that; some don't. If the bitterness bothers you, you could also substitute another kind of green that's more to your liking.

½ cup extra-virgin olive oil

8 fresh garlic cloves, smashed

3 anchovy fillets, whole

Pinch of crushed red-pepper flakes

Sea salt, for pasta water

1 pound orecchiette

One bunch broccoli rabe, woody stems removed

1 ounce Parmigiano Reggiano, grated

Homemade Toasted Bread Crumbs (page 34)

In a medium sauté pan, heat the olive oil, add the garlic, and brown. Add the anchovies and red-pepper flakes. Meanwhile, in a medium stockpot, boil salted water and cook the orecchiette until al dente. When the pasta is almost cooked, add the broccoli rabe to the boiling water. When the pasta is al dente and the broccoli rabe is cooked, add 3 ounces of the hot pasta water to the sauté pan, then strain the pasta and rabe in a colander and add to the pan; toss until well blended. Divide among four bowls and garnish with freshly grated Parmigiano Reggiano and the bread crumbs.

MARTORANO MAC AND CHEESE

SERVES 4

I started making mac and cheese for the kids who'd come into my restaurants with their parents, but found that the **adults, especially ballplayers, love it, too.**

Sea salt, for pasta water

1 pound elbow or shell macaroni

2 ounces domestic provolone

4½ ounces white cheddar cheese

1 pound Velveeta cheese

2 ounces Italian Fontina cheese

1½ cups heavy cream

1 cup Cheetos

Preheat the oven to 350 degrees F.

In salted, boiling water, cook the macaroni until al dente. Then shock it in cold water to stop the cooking process. Dice up all the cheese into ¼-inch pieces. In a medium saucepan over very low heat, heat the heavy cream. While stirring the cream, add all the cheeses. Cook until they are melted and there are no visual lumps. Be sure to keep the flame low to prevent the cheeses from burning on the bottom, and stir occasionally.

In a food processor, crush the Cheetos into a medium-coarse texture.

Put the cooked macaroni in a bowl, and pour in half of the cheese sauce. Mix until well blended. Add the rest of the cheese sauce, and mix well. Pour into a lasagna pan. Top the macaroni and cheese with the crushed Cheetos, and bake for 8 minutes, or until bubbly and toasted. Divide the pasta among four plates, or serve family-style from the pan.

PASTINA AND BUTTER

SERVES 4

My mom made this for me when I was a baby—**my first macaroni.** Today, it's still one of my all-time favorites. There's something comforting going on here that appeals to kids, but also to adults who want that little taste of their childhood.

Sea salt, for pasta water

1 pound pastina

6 ounces salted butter, cut into ½-inch pieces

4 ounces Parmigiano Reggiano, grated

In a medium stockpot, bring salted water to a boil, and cook the pastina until it's al dente, reserving the cooking water. Meanwhile, put the butter in a bowl; once the pastina is cooked, add 4 tablespoons of the pasta water to the bowl. Strain the pastina through a colander, and add it to the bowl. Add the Parmigiano Reggiano, mix everything together, and serve in four separate bowls.

PAPPARDELLE WITH CREAM SAUCE

SERVES 4 TO 6

The secret to this sauce is to reduce the cream by half and then add the Parmigiano Reggiano at the end. The cheese isn't really meant to be cooked, but that's what you get in some restaurants or if you buy that white crap in a jar from the store. **The cheese needs to come in at the last minute** to give this dish that fresh taste. This is Shaquille O'Neal's favorite dish—he orders it every time he comes to the restaurant.

1 tablespoon salted butter

1 quart heavy cream

1 teaspoon freshly ground black pepper

Sea salt, for pasta water

12 ounces pappardelle

½ cup grated Parmigiano Reggiano

To a large sauté pan over medium heat, add the butter, heavy cream, and pepper, and reduce the cream by half. Meanwhile, in boiling, salted water, cook the pappardelle until al dente, then strain through a colander. Whisk the Parmigiano Reggiano into the cream, and toss the pappardelle into the sauce. Divide the pasta and sauce among four to six plates, or serve on a platter.

PROSCIUTTO-WRAPPED PAPPARDELLE WITH CREAM AND TRUFFLE OIL

SERVES 6

I used to make this dish with real truffles, but it was crazy expensive, and, honestly, I'm not that big of a truffle guy to begin with. I like the taste, but I'm not going to go out of my way for truffles. Thanks to the oil, this version still has that truffle flavor. I also played around with the presentation. Now the dish feels more expensive than it actually is. **It's like you're opening a package,** which makes this a great meal for a special occasion.

3 tablespoons salted butter

26 thin slices prosciutto di Parma

1 quart heavy cream

5 ounces Parmigiano Reggiano, grated, plus more for serving

½ cup green peas

Sea salt, for pasta water

1½ pounds pappardelle

3 egg yolks, beaten

1 ounce truffle oil

Freshly ground black pepper to taste

In a large sauté pan, melt the butter. Take two slices of prosciutto, cut them into medium-sized pieces, and add to the pan on low heat. Cook for 1 or 2 minutes. Next add the heavy cream, turn the heat to medium, and cook until the cream is reduced by half. The sauce should be thick enough to coat the back of the spoon. Then add the Parmigiano Reggiano and the peas. Set aside.

In boiling salted water, cook the pappardelle until al dente, strain it through a colander, and place it in a bowl. Add the yolks to the pasta, and toss. Add the pasta to the cream mixture, toss with truffle oil, and season with pepper.

On each of six dinner plates, lay down four slices prosciutto, leaving at least 1 inch of the slices hanging off the rim of the dish. Divide the pasta among the plates, setting it in the middle, on top of the prosciutto. Fold in the ends of the prosciutto to wrap the pasta inside. Garnish each plate with freshly grated Parmigiano Reggiano.

PASTA WITH PEAS AND ONION

SERVES 4

In my restaurants, **we use fresh English peas for this dish.** But when I was growing up, my mother used canned peas. You can use either—or even frozen peas. Fresh peas will give the dish a brighter color, but if you're like me, canned peas will make it taste more like home.

⅓ cup extra-virgin olive oil

4 garlic cloves, smashed

Pinch of crushed red-pepper flakes

½ yellow onion, finely diced

¾ cup chicken stock

6 tablespoons butter, dredged in all-purpose flour

¼ cup green peas

Sea salt, for pasta water

8 ounces tubetti

2 ounces Parmigiano Reggiano, grated

In a large sauté pan, heat the olive oil and cook the garlic until it is brown. Next add the red-pepper flakes and onion, and continue cooking until the onion is translucent. Add the chicken stock, butter dredged in flour, and peas. Cook, allowing the sauce to simmer and thicken. Meanwhile, in a medium pot, boil salted water and cook the tubetti until al dente. Drain the pasta in a colander, then add it to the sauce, tossing and coating the macaroni. Divide the pasta and sauce among four plates. Garnish the pasta with freshly grated Parmigiano Reggiano.

SPAGHETTI AND CRABS

SERVES 4 TO 6

Friday night in the summer, down the Shore, in Wildwood, New Jersey, spaghetti and crabs is a ritual. **When I was young, we always caught the crabs ourselves,** and if you're able to do the same, this dish will taste even better because you'll be freaking hungry. Most of the people I know don't bother to eat the crabs: it's a lot of work for too little meat. But it makes a terrific gravy.

12 live Maryland blue crabs

¼ cup extra-virgin olive oil

1 cup whole garlic cloves, smashed

One 6-ounce can tomato paste

One 28-ounce can San Marzano whole tomatoes, hand crushed

Kosher salt and freshly ground black pepper to taste

Granulated garlic to taste

Sea salt, for pasta water

1 pound spaghetti

To clean a crab, pry off the top shell, killing the crab instantly. Next, flip the crab over, remove the apron and the gills, and then rinse it under cold water. Repeat this process for each crab. In a large stockpot, heat the olive oil and sauté the garlic until it is golden brown. Add the cleaned crabs, and sauté for 3 or 4 minutes, until the crabs have changed to a reddish color. Add the tomato paste, and coat the crabs with it. Now add the San Marzano tomatoes, season with salt, pepper, and granulated garlic, and cook, covered, for 20 minutes, stirring occasionally.

In a separate pot, bring salted water to a boil, and cook the spaghetti until al dente. Strain the pasta through a colander, and add to the crab gravy. Toss well in the pot; divide the crabs, sauce, and pasta among four to six bowls, or serve on a platter.

RIGATONI TRIPE PARMESAN

SERVES 4

My father would make this for his friends when they went to the Poconos on weekend hunting trips. They hardly ever came home with anything, but they ate well.

3½ pound honeycomb tripe

¼ cup extra-virgin olive oil

7 garlic cloves, smashed

2 carrots, finely diced

3 stalks celery, finely diced

Two 28-ounce cans San Marzano
    whole tomatoes

Salt and freshly ground black pepper
    to taste

8 fresh basil leaves, torn

3 ounces Parmigiano Reggiano,
    grated, plus more for serving

Sea salt, for pasta water

1 pound rigatoni

In a medium pot, bring water to a boil. If the tripe is frozen, defrost it in cool running water. Boil the tripe for 1½ to 2 hours, or until it is tender. To check for doneness, insert a fork: when you get no resistance, remove the tripe from the water and allow it to cool. When it is cool to the touch, cut the tripe into ½-inch pieces.

In a medium saucepan, heat the olive oil and brown the garlic, then add the carrots and celery, and sauté for 3 minutes. Crush the San Marzano tomatoes by hand, and add them to the pot along with the tripe. Season with salt and pepper, cover, and cook for 10 minutes. Add the fresh basil and Parmigiano Reggiano.

In a separate pot, boil salted water, add the rigatoni, and cook until al dente. Strain through a colander and toss the pasta into the tripe sauce. Divide the pasta and sauce among four plates, or serve on a platter. Garnish with freshly grated Parmigiano Reggiano.

STROZZAPRETI WITH CAULIFLOWER

SERVES 4 TO 6

Strozzapreti—a cut of macaroni that's a little thinner, longer, and less common in America than cavatelli—means "priest strangler" or "priest choker" in Italian. Supposedly, strozzapreti got its name because **priests found the macaroni so delicious that they stuffed themselves until they choked.**

Sea salt, for pasta water

20 ounces strozzapreti

¾ cup extra-virgin olive oil

12 garlic cloves, smashed and chopped

8 anchovy fillets, whole

½ cup raisins

½ cup toasted pine nuts

Pinch of crushed red-pepper flakes

1 head cauliflower, stemmed

Bring a large pot of salted water to a boil, and start to cook the strozzapreti.

Meanwhile, in a hot sauté pan, heat the olive oil, and sauté the garlic until it is almost brown. Add the anchovies and melt them into the oil. Add the raisins, pine nuts, red-pepper flakes, and 2 tablespoons of the pasta water. When the macaroni has been cooking for 11 minutes, add the cauliflower to the sauté pan. Strain the pasta through a colander, and add the strozzapreti to the pan. Cook the pasta and cauliflower for an additional 4 minutes, or until both are tender. Toss well, divide evenly among plates, and serve.

SPAGHETTI LOBSTER FRA DIAVOLO

SERVES 4

Maine lobster can be expensive—and for some people, it can even be a once-in-a-lifetime experience. That's why I think **it's important to make the most of lobster.** After you steam the lobster, keep it in its shell. That way, nothing goes to waste, and you'll get a ton of flavor.

Two 2½-pound live Maine lobsters

Sea salt, for boiling lobsters and pasta water

¼ cup extra-virgin olive oil

8 garlic cloves, smashed

12 ounces San Marzano whole tomatoes, hand crushed

½ teaspoon kosher salt

¼ teaspoon freshly ground black pepper

½ teaspoon granulated garlic

4 fresh basil leaves, torn

¼ teaspoon dried oregano

¼ teaspoon crushed red-pepper flakes

1 pound spaghetti

1 cup Homemade Toasted Bread Crumbs (recipe on page 34)

Put one of the lobsters on a clean cutting board. While holding the lobster, take a sharp knife and cut it in half, starting at the head, so it will die instantly. Repeat with the second lobster.

Bring salted water to a boil in a large pot, and cook the lobsters for 10 minutes, then remove from the water, allow to cool, and set aside. Reserve the water for later. When the lobsters are cool to the touch, remove the meat from the shells.

In a sauté pan, heat the olive oil and brown the smashed garlic. Then add the San Marzano tomatoes, and season with the salt, black pepper, granulated garlic, basil, oregano, and red-pepper flakes. Cook on medium-high heat for 5 minutes. Add the lobster meat to the sauce and simmer the sauce until the meat is firm and white.

Add salt to the water that you poached the lobster in, and bring it back to a boil. Cook your spaghetti until al dente, strain, and toss into the sauce. Put the pasta in a serving dish, place sauce and meat on top, and garnish with toasted bread crumbs.

SUNDAY PORK GRAVY WITH RIGATONI

SERVES 8

You can buy a thousand different kinds and brands of tomatoes, but **I only use tomatoes from the San Marzano area of Italy.** To me, they taste the best. How do I know what I'm buying? The cans of real San Marzano tomatoes are stamped or labeled "DOP." That's an acronym that stands for *"Denominazione di Origine Protetta."* DOP is a certification that ensures that the product you're buying is the real thing.

2 pounds boneless pork butt, cut into 2-inch cubes

1 pound pigs' feet, split in half

¼ pound fatback

1½ tablespoons kosher salt, plus more to taste

1½ teaspoons freshly ground black pepper, plus more to taste

1½ tablespoons granulated garlic, plus more to taste

½ cup extra-virgin olive oil

1 medium yellow onion, diced

¼ cup whole garlic cloves, smashed

Four 28-ounce cans San Marzano whole tomatoes, hand-crushed

8 fresh basil leaves, torn

2 cups grated Parmigiano Reggiano

Sea salt, for pasta water

2 pounds rigatoni

¼ cup grated Pecorino Romano

1 cup ricotta impastata

Evenly coat the pork butt, pigs' feet, and fatback with the salt, pepper, and granulated garlic. Heat a medium Dutch oven over medium-high heat, and add the olive oil, pork butt, pigs' feet, fatback, and onion. Brown the meats on all sides; then add the smashed garlic, and cook until it is brown. Turn the flame down to medium-low, add the crushed San Marzano tomatoes, and cover. Stir periodically, allowing nothing to stick to the bottom of the pot. After approximately 2½ hours, or when the meat is tender, add the basil and Parmigiano Reggiano, and simmer for an additional 15 minutes. Season with salt, black pepper, and granulated garlic.

In a separate pot, boil salted water and cook the rigatoni until al dente. As the pasta cooks, remove the pigs' feet from the gravy, and discard. Strain the pasta through a colander, and toss with the gravy. Divide evenly among eight plates, garnish with Pecorino Romano and a dollop of ricotta impastata, and serve.

YO CUZ!

STRUGGLE

BY THE LATE 1970S, my career as a DJ was starting to progress. That winter, I got my big break after a job that didn't pan out led me to a chance meeting with Giuseppe "Joe" Gambino. He was one of three Sicilian brothers known as "the Cherry Hill Gambinos," part of the New York crime family. Joe and his brother Sal ran Valentino's, a Cherry Hill, New Jersey, nightclub that was one of the hottest spots in the Philadelphia area. It wasn't long before I'd become a regular DJ there.

At Valentino's—a place with girls in dresses, guys in suits, and big fellas at the door speaking in Italian—there were only two smells: food and cologne. Guys wore that shit by the bottle. I was no different, except I never liked people to know what I was wearing, and if they figured it out, I'd switch, or I'd start mixing the stuff—a little from this bottle, a little from that one. I didn't like the idea of guys in my crew using the same cologne. Plus, it kept the ladies guessing, which always presented the opportunity for a good pickup line.

"Steve, what are you wearing?" they'd ask. And I'd say, "It's called Come Follow Me." This worked like a charm, and being the club DJ didn't hurt, either. There were all kinds of girls around, willing to climb into the booth with me and fool around. I'd just play an extra-long version of something, and no one on the dance floor below had a clue.

> **Every day may not be good, but there's something good in every day.**

ABOVE *My dad, me winning DJ of the year award, and my mom*

As far as the food was concerned, Valentino's wasn't Sunday dinner at Gram's house, but it wasn't bad. Joe and Sal had a kitchenful of Italians immigrants working the line. During breaks or after my shift, I loved to hang out and watch the Zips cook. Zips were what we called guys that came from *It-lee*. They made veal piccata, veal Marsala, and chicken and peppers—all good, but nothing as good as I could get at home or make myself. I'd always wondered why food at a restaurant didn't taste quite as good as food at home, and now I began to see why: precooked cutlets and macaroni, and products, such as olive oil, that were good but not the best.

One night, I blew the minds of the guys in the kitchen when I cooked veal piccata and made sandwiches out of it with a double order of veal with lots of lemon flavor. "What kind of DJ cooks like this?" they asked. "The Italian-American kind," I told them, and they cursed me in Italian. It was great.

On another occasion, Mr. Bruno, the boss of the Philly Family, and Uncle Raymond came to Valentino's for dinner. I had remembered that my aunt Evelyn, Raymond's wife, once told me Angelo loved linguine and clams with prosciutto, so I went into the kitchen and decided to surprise him.

Angelo, himself a first-generation Sicilian, took a bite. Then Mr. Bruno leaned back in his chair, touched the bridge of his thick glasses frames, and smiled.

"Who cooked this?" Angelo asked Raymond.

I stepped forward and boasted, "No cook, just a DJ."

Mr. Bruno smiled.

Being in the kitchen felt natural. But never in a million years did I think I'd go from veal sandwiches to cooking linguine and clams with prosciutto for Angelo Bruno, to my mind the most powerful man in Philadelphia. And even though I continued to concentrate on my music, that experience with Mr. Bruno encouraged me to make more regular visits to the restaurant kitchen. It was a spark.

"What kind of DJ cooks like this?" they asked. "The Italian-American kind," I told them, and they cursed me in Italian. It was great.

ABOVE *Me DJing at Valentino's*

ABOUT A YEAR after I'd been hired by the Gambinos, I hooked up with a girl bartender of theirs. After shutting down the club one night, we went to a diner across the street for something to eat, and later got a room, where I knocked her goofy. Early the next morning, I drove the girl back to her car. Almost immediately, we were surrounded by three other cars.

It's a hit, I thought.

"Oh, shit," she said. "It's John."

"Who the fuck is John?"

Then a guy got out of one of the cars, ordered the girl inside, and gave me a warning:

"Stay the fuck away from my girl or you'll get your legs broke."

I didn't know how many other guys were in the cars or if this guy had a gun, so I played it safe and took off.

When I got home, I was concerned about what had happened and prepared for the worst. I called my friend Anthony and told him the story.

"Listen," I told Anthony, "we gotta be ready for these guys tonight if they show up again. I'll be holding. Make sure you've got something, too."

My father called me downstairs. He had been at home, recovering from a work accident–a twelve-hundred-pound fence fell on him while he was making deliveries, leaving him with two broken legs, laid up in a body cast, and confined to bed. He was resting in the parlor and heard every word of my conversation with Anthony on the extension.

> **"Listen," I told Anthony, "we gotta be ready for these guys tonight if they show up again. I'll be holding. Make sure you've got something, too."**

"Son, what do you need a fucking gun for?" he said.

I told him the story and asked him not to say anything to Uncle Raymond. He was furious. I didn't want to get him upset because of his condition, but what could I do? He was my father. He told me he would take care of it. Still, I left for work with my piece.

I wasn't at the club long before Angelo Bruno walked through the door with one of his lieutenants, Sonny Riccobene, and my uncle.

"Where's Joe Gambino?" Angelo demanded. "Where's Sal?"

The men sat in the back of the restaurant and talked about what had happened with me and the girl. Fifteen minutes later, Joe Gambino arrived and went over to their table.

Joe knew the girl's boyfriend, John. He knew where he lived.

The next day, Uncle Raymond sent two of his men to the boyfriend's house. They knocked on the door, and his wife answered. She tried to bluff and acted like he wasn't at home, but it didn't take Raymond's men long to find him. They held a gun to his head, dragged him out of the house, and shoved him into the backseat of a car. When they got to John's Vending, they dragged the guy into Raymond's office. Then the boyfriend crawled to where Raymond was sitting.

I realized Uncle Raymond might raise his hand, but he didn't need to lower it to be feared.

"Jesus!" he cried. "Please–don't kill me. I'm in love with her. God– don't kill me. I saw her with your nephew and I was jealous. I'm sorry. I'm sorry. I'll leave. I'll leave her, leave the country–whatever you want. Just don't kill me."

"Be careful who you threaten," Uncle Raymond said.

And just like that, they let the boyfriend go. I realized Uncle Raymond might raise his hand, but he didn't need to lower it to be feared.

BY THE EARLY 1980S, South Philly was a dangerous place, and I was heading down the wrong path. The incident with the boyfriend was just one episode, but there were many others.

At one point while I was doing the DJ thing, Joey and I got the bright idea that we were going to sell drugs out of the clubs to make a little extra money. Back then, pills were part of the culture, but that's not an excuse–I was stupid. On top of that, I wasn't a great businessman.

The plan was simple: my cousin was going to front the pills and take 30 percent, and then Joey and I would split the rest. We hooked up with a Zip named Joe to deal half of the stuff. But after only twenty-four hours, Joe the Italian had disappeared, along with the pills and any chance of making back our money.

"It'll be all right," said Joey. "He's your cousin. He'll understand."

To make up for the loss, we brought our half of the pills to a joint called the London Victory Club in Center City, where I was also working at the time. At work that night, I gave the pills to Anthony. He was supposed to take care of business, but at some point during the night I walked out of the club and saw people running in the middle of the street. I walked over and saw Anthony. He was on his hands and knees and all fucked up. He had dropped the bag of pills in the street, and people were diving for them. I saw that there were cops all over the place, and I left.

The next morning, when I went looking for Anthony, he didn't have any money. I thought about smacking him, but where would that get me? I decided to deal with him later. Then I went to my cousin and told him the story.

"What the fuck do you want me to do?"

"What the fuck do you want *me* to do?" said my cousin.

"Cuz, you're my fucking cousin. Come on, cuz, help me out here."

"Help you out, cuz? It's business." He shrugged. "It's got nothing to do with us being cousins."

He was my cousin. I loved him. But none of that mattered. I needed money to pay him back. Playing clubs a few nights a week wasn't going to be enough. I needed a part-time job, so I went to my father.

ANTON'S WAS A SOUTH PHILLY JOINT at the corner of 11th and Ellsworth. It had a sign out front, a kitchen in the tiny basement, and a second floor for parties that was used more often for storage and talking family business. As far as the city was concerned, the bar belonged to my father. In reality, it was Uncle Raymond's place, and my father was simply an employee. Soon enough, I was, too.

When the casinos first opened in Atlantic City, people were flocking down to the Shore as fast as they could print money. Even with illegal poker machines, Anton's couldn't attract new business, and its clientele was stale. Old-timers formed a line at the door before we opened in the morning and usually stayed until 4:00 or 5:00 p.m., doing their daily bullshit, like taking numbers and borrowing money. They sat on the stools and played cards between rounds of Cutty Sark and Rolling Rock.

My father and I didn't see eye to eye on a lot of things, and running Anton's was one of them.

My father, who had never quite recovered from his work accident, limped from customer to customer as they called out for their drinks.

My father and I didn't see eye to eye on a lot of things, and running Anton's was one of them. He was a great guy, but never had the ambition to think big or do something different. He was content to pour beers and shots, and make a few bucks here and there. I wanted real money. We argued, but he was stubborn.

Like everything else I tried in South Philly, working at Anton's seemed a dead end. I just hadn't seen the potential—yet.

I started to get the idea that Anton's could be something more than just a neighborhood bar—that my father and I could make more money if we took a little risk. Only, this time, I didn't really tell my father about my idea.

Like everything else I tried in South Philly, working at Anton's seemed a dead end. I just hadn't seen the potential—yet.

On most mornings, before Anton's opened, I put credits in the poker machines without paying, and played until I hit. I began putting the money aside to buy things for the bar—usually pots, pans, and quality Italian food products. I never spent the money on myself. It wasn't long before my father figured out the scam, but by that time I'd gotten what I needed to upgrade the bar's kitchen. Then I started thinking big.

One of my cousins, Ronnie Durante, had recently opened Philadelphia's first video store—South Philly Video, at 11th and Oregon. I took some of my poker winnings and bought one of Ronnie's big-ass video machines and picked up a few movies. I was going to put on a *Godfather* night at the bar. Playing a movie in a restaurant or bar had never been done before, as far as I knew. I was just trying to be original. I knew people loved food. I knew they loved *The Godfather*. Why not combine the two? And with a great jukebox? It seemed like a no-brainer.

Then, when the movie was over and the credits began to roll, people stood and clapped.

I explained the idea to my father—we'd hold an all-you-can-eat spaghetti-and-crabs night and offer entertainment for $9.95. Dinner and a show—just like Atlantic City. I showed him the VCR. He wasn't impressed, and clung to the idea that people weren't going to come to the bar for anything but a drink or two. Still, I wore him down, and he gave me a chance to prove him wrong. I started to put up fliers all over South Philly.

The afternoon before the big night, I began cooking, then went about cleaning the bar from top to bottom. A few of the old-timers blew me shit

("What's with all that cleaning? You some kind of sissy?"). They didn't think Anton's could be anything but a bar, either.

But when five o'clock rolled around, the place was packed, and a line to get in was beginning to form. I popped the movie into the VCR, and the night was off and running. Everything went well—the food was great and the restaurant was full—but the customers were quiet. Honestly, I was starting to get a little worried. Plus, I saw the look on my father's face: despite the crowd, he was still skeptical. Then, when the movie was over and the credits began to roll, people stood and clapped. As the people cheered, my father pulled me aside and whispered:

"What are we showing next week, son?"

YO CUZ!

ENTRÉES

CHICKEN CUTLET BROCCOLI RABE

SERVES 4

The key to this recipe is to **start with a thin chicken breast.** My mom used to pound the chicken breasts between pieces of waxed paper with a meat mallet, but you could just as easily ask your butcher to do it for you. That's the difference between a good cutlet and a great one.

Four 6-ounce skinless, boneless chicken breast halves, pounded thin

¼ teaspoon kosher salt

¼ teaspoon freshly ground black pepper

¼ teaspoon granulated garlic

All-purpose flour, for dredging

Vegetable oil, for frying

2 tablespoons extra-virgin olive oil

4 garlic cloves

2 anchovy fillets, whole

One bunch broccoli rabe, woody stems removed

½ cup chicken stock

¼ teaspoon crushed red-pepper flakes

2 ounces sharp provolone, sliced

EGG WASH

3 eggs

½ teaspoon kosher salt

½ teaspoon freshly ground black pepper

¼ cup finely chopped fresh Italian parsley

¼ cup grated Parmigiano Reggiano

BREAD-CRUMB MIXTURE

2 cups unseasoned bread crumbs

¼ cup finely chopped fresh Italian parsley

¼ cup grated Parmigiano Reggiano

TO MAKE THE EGG WASH Crack the eggs into a medium bowl, and add the salt, pepper, parsley, and Parmigiano Reggiano. Whisk together until well blended. In a separate bowl, mix the bread crumbs, parsley, and Parmigiano Reggiano until well combined, and set aside.

On a separate plate, season the chicken on both sides with the salt, pepper, and granulated garlic. Dredge each cutlet in the flour, shaking off the excess. Dip each cutlet into the egg wash, and then coat in the bread-crumb mixture. Repeat until all the chicken is breaded, making sure the chicken is fully coated. In a large sauté pan, heat the vegetable oil and carefully add the chicken; fry one cutlet at a time until both sides are golden brown.

Meanwhile, heat a sauté pan with the olive oil, brown the garlic, and add the anchovies. Place the broccoli rabe in the pan, along with the chicken stock and red-pepper flakes, and cook for 4 minutes, or until the broccoli rabe is tender. Divide the chicken cutlets and broccoli rabe among four plates, top with slices of provolone cheese, and serve.

CHICKEN CUTLET **MARSALA**

SERVES 4

This would also work great with veal or pork cutlets. If you want a slightly earthier flavor, substitute wild mushrooms, or a mix of creminis, shiitakes, and porcinis, for the button mushrooms.

Four 6-ounce skinless, boneless chicken breast halves, pounded thin

¼ teaspoon kosher salt

¼ teaspoon freshly ground black pepper

¼ teaspoon granulated garlic

All-purpose flour, for dredging

1 cup vegetable oil, for frying

6 ounces Italian Fontina, sliced

SAUCE

1 tablespoon butter

3 cups fresh button mushrooms, chopped

Kosher salt and freshly ground pepper

Granulated garlic

¼ cup dry Marsala wine

½ cup chicken stock

EGG WASH

3 eggs

½ teaspoon kosher salt

½ teaspoon freshly ground black pepper

¼ cup finely chopped fresh Italian parsley

¼ cup grated Parmigiano Reggiano

BREAD-CRUMB MIXTURE

2 cups unseasoned bread crumbs

¼ cup finely chopped fresh Italian parsley

¼ cup grated Parmigiano Reggiano

TO MAKE THE EGG WASH Crack the eggs into a medium bowl, and add the salt, pepper, parsley, and Parmigiano Reggiano. Whisk together until well blended. In a separate bowl, mix the bread crumbs, parsley, and Parmigiano Reggiano until well combined, and set aside.

Preheat the oven to 350 degrees F.

On a separate plate, season the chicken on both sides with the salt, pepper, and granulated garlic. Dredge each cutlet in the flour, shaking off the excess. Dip each cutlet into the egg wash, and then coat in the bread-crumb mixture. Repeat until all the chicken is breaded, making sure the chicken is fully coated. In a large sauté pan, heat the vegetable oil and carefully add the chicken; fry one cutlet at a time until both sides are golden brown.

TO MAKE THE MARSALA SAUCE heat a small sauté pan with butter. Add the mushrooms, season with salt, pepper, and granulated garlic, and sauté them until they are brown and cooked (soft). Deglaze the pan with the Marsala, then add the chicken stock. Cook until the sauce reduces by half, 5 to 6 minutes.

While the sauce is cooking, place a slice of Fontina cheese on each cutlet on a baking sheet, and bake for 3 minutes, or until the cheese is melted. Take the chicken out of the oven, and divide among four plates. Remove the sauce from the heat, spoon it over the cutlets, and serve.

CHICKEN ON THE BONE

SERVES 4

If you want to do something different here, you could just as easily substitute rabbit for the chicken. Either way, this makes for a hearty dinner—**a great dish for the winter.**

2 cups vegetable oil

2 chicken thighs

2 chicken drumsticks

½ teaspoon kosher salt, plus more for sauce

½ teaspoon freshly ground black pepper, plus more for sauce

½ teaspoon granulated garlic, plus more for sauce

4 ounces hot sausage

4 ounces sweet sausage

½ cup extra-virgin olive oil

2 cups button mushrooms, sliced

1 small yellow onion, julienned

1 small red bell pepper, stemmed, seeded, and cut into ¼-inch pieces

1 small yellow bell pepper, stemmed, seeded, and cut into ¼-inch pieces

¼ cup Pinot Grigio

¾ cup chicken stock

7 ounces San Marzano whole tomatoes, hand-crushed

1 bunch Italian parsley, coarsely chopped

Preheat the oven to 350 degrees F. In a 14-inch, deep sauté pan, heat the vegetable oil until hot but not smoking. Season the chicken with the salt, black pepper, and granulated garlic. Place the chicken in the hot oil, skin side down, taking care not to splash the oil. Cook the chicken, allowing it to brown on one side. Turn the chicken over, and add the hot and sweet sausage. Allow the other side of the chicken and the sausage to brown.

Drain out the oil and discard. Return the pan with the chicken and sausage to the stove over medium heat, and add the olive oil. Gently add the mushrooms, onion, and peppers to the pan, sautéing them until tender. Remove the pan from the heat, and deglaze with the Pinot Grigio. Return the pan to the heat, and add the chicken stock, San Marzano tomatoes, parsley, and salt, black pepper, and granulated garlic to taste.

Cover, and cook in the oven for 20 minutes, or until the chicken reaches 165 degrees F inside. Remove the cover, place the pan back on the stovetop, and reduce the sauce over medium heat until it becomes thick and coats the back of a spoon. Add the chicken and sauce to a platter and serve family style.

CLASSIC PIZZA

MAKES 1 PIZZA, SERVING 4

The secret to making quality pizza at home is your oven temperature. **Set your oven to 550 degrees F and preheat it for at least an hour.** A pizza stone also works great. When you use one, make sure you put the stone on one of the highest racks in your oven, but leave enough room for the pizza. Also, if you get a pizza stone, you're going to need a wooden pizza peel. You can find both the stone and the peel in specialty stores that sell cooking tools and equipment.

4 ounces San Marzano whole tomatoes

¼ teaspoon kosher salt

¼ teaspoon freshly ground black pepper

1 ball Pizza Dough (recipe follows)

All-purpose flour, for the work surface

Cornmeal, for the pizza peel

¼ teaspoon granulated garlic

3 ounces Fresh Mozzarella (page 29), grated

2 tablespoons grated Pecorino Romano

2 tablespoons grated Parmigiano Reggiano, plus more for serving

3 tablespoons extra-virgin olive oil

2 tablespoons torn fresh basil leaves

Pinch of dried oregano

Preheat the oven to 550 degrees F.

In a food processor, purée the San Marzano tomatoes for 10 to 15 seconds. Season with the salt and pepper and set aside.

Place the pizza dough on a well-floured surface, and push the dough down with the tips of your fingers. Next, with a rolling pin, roll out the dough, starting from the middle and working outward, until it is 12 inches in diameter. Dust a pizza peel with cornmeal, and put the rolled-out dough on it.

Season the dough with the granulated garlic, and spoon two heaping spoonfuls of the puréed tomatoes in the middle of the dough. Using the back of your spoon, spread the sauce in a circular motion, spreading it outward and allowing a ¼-inch rim for the crust. Top the dough with mozzarella, Pecorino Romano, Parmigiano Reggiano, and your favorite toppings. Drizzle the olive oil on top of the pie, and bake on a pizza stone for 12 to 14 minutes. Be sure to rotate the dough halfway through the baking time, to ensure even cooking. When it's fully browned and cooked, remove it from the oven. Top with torn fresh basil, dried oregano, and freshly grated Parmigiano Reggiano.

PIZZA DOUGH

MAKES 7 DOUGH BALLS

Caputo is a brand of Italian flour, and "00" is the type you need for pizza dough. The number—also called *doppio zero* in Italian—refers to the fact that the flour is ground to a fine powder (the higher the number, the coarser the grind). Caputo "00"—which produces strong and elastic dough—is similar to American pastry or cake flour. Caputo might be a little hard to find in stores, but it's available online in a number of places. Is it necessary? Probably not, but it's definitely the right choice for those wanting to produce an authentic Italian pie.

7 cups Caputo "00" flour, plus more for dusting

1½ tablespoons kosher salt

1 tablespoon instant dry yeast

2 tablespoons extra-virgin olive oil

4 cups water

Place the flour, salt, yeast, and olive oil in a mixer with a dough hook. Turn it on at medium speed (number 2 or 3). As the hook turns slowly, add three-quarters of the water slowly, and as the dough ball forms, slowly and continuously add the rest of the water. Add enough water so the flour forms a large ball. As you continue to add the water, you will notice that the dough starts to stick to the sides of the bowl. Keep mixing for 2 or 3 minutes. When the dough starts to come away from the sides of the bowl, it is ready. Flour your hands, and place the dough on a floured surface.

With a knife, portion the ball into 7 pieces. Tuck each piece of dough inside itself, forming it into a tight ball, and place them all on a floured sheet pan. Cover with plastic wrap or a wet towel, and allow to rest for 1 hour prior to baking. Unused dough will last up to 2 days wrapped in the refrigerator, or 3 months stored frozen in a plastic zipper-lock bag.

FRIED CHICKEN

SERVES 4

Paula Deen is a dear friend. A while back, she had me on her TV show, then opened up her home to me and my girlfriend, Marsha Daley. Paula was such a generous and giving host—except when it came to her fried-chicken recipe. That, she wouldn't share, and I don't blame her. When I got back home, I tried to figure out what made hers so fucking great, and I read about a dozen recipes to find out what they all had in common. **I think the secret's in her black cast-iron skillet**—one of those old-school things that just work.

8 chicken thighs, bone in, skin on

2 teaspoons kosher salt, plus more for marinating

2 teaspoons freshly ground black pepper, plus more for marinating

2 teaspoons granulated garlic, plus more for marinating

3 cups buttermilk

3 quarts vegetable oil

4 cups all-purpose flour

½ teaspoon MSG

4 tablespoons butter

On a clean plate, season the chicken with salt, pepper, and granulated garlic. Place in a bowl, cover completely with the buttermilk, and allow to sit in the refrigerator overnight.

In a 6-quart pot or large cast-iron pan, heat the vegetable oil to 350 degrees F. (Use a candy thermometer to gauge the correct temperature.) Meanwhile, in a medium bowl, mix the flour, 2 teaspoons salt, 2 teaspoons pepper, 2 teaspoons granulated garlic, and the MSG until well blended.

Take the chicken out of the buttermilk mixture and put it on a separate plate, shaking off the excess. One piece at a time, place the chicken in the flour mixture, push the flour onto the chicken, shake off the excess, and place the chicken on another plate. Repeat this process until all the chicken is coated with the flour.

When the oil reaches 350 degrees F, carefully place the floured chicken, one piece at a time, into the hot oil. Cook the chicken all together, but do not overcrowd your pan. (If your pan isn't large enough, work in batches.) The chicken takes roughly 20 minutes to cook. When 15 minutes have elapsed, take the largest piece of chicken and insert a thermometer inside, next to, but not touching, the bone. Once the internal temperature has reached 160 degrees F, remove the chicken from the oil, place it on a wire rack, and allow it to rest for 3 minutes. Divide the chicken evenly among four plates, top each piece with 1½ teaspoons butter, and serve.

HOT DOGS AND PEPPERS

SERVES 4

My mother made this when I was a kid, and **you could feel the love when you were eating it.**
It's not a fancy dish, but it's comforting. At its best, I think that's what Italian-American cooking—
like peasant food—is all about.

6 hot dogs

2 tablespoons extra-virgin olive oil

3 garlic cloves, smashed

1 yellow onion, julienned

1 small red bell pepper, stemmed,
  seeded, and cut into ¼-inch pieces

1 small yellow bell pepper, stemmed,
  seeded, and cut into ¼-inch pieces

Kosher salt and freshly ground black
  pepper

Granulated garlic

One 28-ounce can San Marzano
  whole tomatoes, hand crushed

2 tablespoons torn fresh basil

½ cup grated Parmigiano Reggiano

Italian bread (optional)

Cut the hot dogs on the diagonal into 1-inch pieces. In a medium sauté pan, heat the olive oil and add the garlic, cooking it until it is golden brown. Add the onion and peppers, and sauté them until tender. Season with a pinch each of salt, black pepper, and granulated garlic. Add the hot dogs, and cook over medium heat for about 15 minutes. Add the crushed tomatoes, and season with more salt, black pepper, granulated garlic, and add the basil. Cover, and cook over medium heat for 20 minutes. Remove from the heat, add the Parmigiano Reggiano, and mix until incorporated. Can be served in a bowl, or on an Italian roll as a sandwich.

PORK CHOP MARTORANO

SERVES 4

In the restaurant world, people think thicker means better; it's all about presentation. But sometimes that's a bunch of bullshit. **I like a thin chop—less than ¼ inch thick.** It takes just 8 minutes to cook, and you can dress it up with hot cherry peppers and a little of the brine. You can make your money go a little further, and your stomach won't know the difference.

Four 8-ounce center-cut pork chops

2 teaspoons kosher salt

2 teaspoons freshly ground black pepper

2 teaspoons granulated garlic

2 tablespoons extra-virgin olive oil

SAUCE

1 ounce extra-virgin olive oil

2 garlic cloves, chopped

1 ounce Pinot Grigio

½ cup chicken stock

1 teaspoon salted butter

½ teaspoon all-purpose flour

4 cherry peppers, plus ½ ounce juice

GARNISH

One bunch prepared broccoli rabe (see page 23)

2 ounces sharp provolone, sliced

Preheat the oven to 375 degrees F.

On a plate, season the pork chops with the salt, pepper, and granulated garlic. Heat a large ovenproof sauté pan with the olive oil, and pan-sear both sides of each chop until golden brown. Then place in the oven, and bake for 15 to 20 minutes. Set aside.

To make the sauce, heat a small sauté pan with the olive oil, and brown the garlic. Deglaze the pan with the wine, and add the chicken stock, butter, flour, and cherry peppers with their juices; reduce until thick. Place each pork chop on a plate, and top with broccoli rabe and sauce, divided evenly. Top each with slices of sharp provolone cheese, and serve.

CLAMS MARTORANO

SERVES 4

I grew up hanging out with my cousin Georgie. As Uncle Raymond's son, he was the prince of South Philly, and I used to love going out on the town with him, especially to The Saloon, a neighborhood bar that had great food. The Saloon drew a great crowd—politicians, gangsters, doctors, and blue-collar guys—and having dinner there with Georgie was always a great time. **He was the kind of guy everyone loved, and, just like his dad, he always looked sharp.** I swear to God, Georgie would change his shoes four times a day. We used to order the same thing every time, clams Pavarotti. Today, Georgie is in prison on a bullshit charge, but I stay in close touch and think of him all the time—especially when I make my version of this great dish.

¼ cup extra-virgin olive oil

1 stalk celery, chopped

¼ onion, chopped

4 ounces shrimp

4 ounces lump crabmeat

One recipe Béchamel Sauce (recipe follows)

1 sprig fresh thyme

2 teaspoons all-purpose flour

2 teaspoons bread crumbs

4 cleaned clamshells

Make the Béchamel Sauce and set aside.

Preheat the oven to 375 degrees F. Heat a medium sauté pan with the olive oil. When the oil is hot, add the celery and onion, and sauté them for 3 minutes. Next, add the shrimp and crabmeat, and cook for 3 minutes. Then add hot béchamel slowly to the pan; strip off the thyme leaves, add them, and cook for an additional 2 minutes. Thicken the sauce with the flour and bread crumbs. Continue cooking until it reduces—it should be thick, not soupy. Let the mixture cool on a sheet pan or a dish. When it is cool to the touch, divide it evenly among clean clamshells. Put them in a pan, and cook for 4 minutes. Top with more béchamel, and bake for another 3 to 4 minutes, or until golden brown.

BÉCHAMEL SAUCE

5 tablespoons butter

¼ cup all-purpose flour

4 cups milk

⅓ cup grated Parmigiano Reggiano

2 teaspoons kosher salt

In a medium saucepan, heat the butter over medium-low heat until melted. Add the flour, and stir until smooth. Cook until the mixture turns a light golden brown, 6 to 7 minutes.

Meanwhile, heat the milk in a separate pan to a simmer. Add the butter mixture to the hot milk, and whisk continuously until very smooth. Bring to a boil, stirring constantly. When the sauce is thick and smooth, remove from heat, and whisk in the Parmigiano Reggiano. Season with the salt.

LOBSTER FRANÇAISE

SERVES 4

Lobster Française was a specialty of The Saloon, a South Philly neighborhood joint. When I was younger, I thought that place was the greatest Italian-American restaurant in the world, and when I started cooking for a living, my goal was to be as good as they were. **This dish is my tribute.**

1 cup vegetable oil

Four 6-ounce South African lobster
    tails

¼ teaspoon kosher salt

¼ teaspoon freshly ground black
    pepper

¼ teaspoon granulated garlic

All-purpose flour, for dredging

EGG BATTER

6 eggs

½ cup finely chopped fresh Italian
    parsley

½ cup grated Parmigiano Reggiano

1 teaspoon granulated garlic

1 teaspoon freshly ground black
    pepper

LEMON BUTTER SAUCE

2 tablespoons Pinot Grigio

¾ cup chicken stock

Juice of ½ lemon

4 ounces lump crabmeat

1 tablespoon butter, coated with all-
    purpose flour

1 tablespoon roughly chopped fresh
    Italian parsley

TO MAKE THE EGG BATTER Crack the eggs into a large bowl, add all the other ingredients, and mix.

In a large sauté pan, heat the vegetable oil to 350 degrees F. (Use a candy thermometer to gauge the correct temperature.) Cut the lobster tails in half lengthwise. Remove the shell, and season the lobster with the salt, pepper, and granulated garlic. Reserve the shells. Coat the seasoned lobster in the flour, and dip it into the egg mixture. You can test the oil by putting some egg batter into the oil; when the egg expands quickly, the oil is ready. With a pair of tongs, remove the lobster from the egg mixture and carefully place each piece into the hot oil. Cook on all sides until golden brown, about 3 minutes per side.

In a separate hot pan, heat the wine and allow the alcohol to burn off. Then add chicken stock, lemon juice, crabmeat, and butter coated with flour. Simmer the sauce until it becomes thick and coats the back of the spoon. Place two half-lobster tails in the center of each of four plates, crisscrossing one another. Place an equal amount of crabmeat on top of the lobster, drizzle with the sauce, and serve.

LEFT *The Saloon, my favorite Italian-American restaurant in South Philly*

LOBSTER MARTORANO

SERVES 6

I always use a cold-water lobster instead of a warm-water one. I like them because the meat is whiter and sweeter, and cuts like butter. Cold-water tails are commonly found from Maine, Australia, New Zealand, and South Africa. Lobsters from these areas will be a little more expensive than warm-water lobsters, but **they're worth the price.**

1 recipe Béchamel Sauce (page 102)

Six 2-pound live Maine lobsters

Sea salt, for boiling lobsters

¼ cup extra-virgin olive oil

8 garlic cloves, chopped

4 stalks celery, diced

1 yellow onion, diced

1 tablespoon finely chopped fresh thyme

1 tablespoon salted butter

8 ounces mushrooms, sliced

¾ cup Parmigiano Reggiano, grated

¾ cup cheddar cheese, grated

Homemade Toasted Bread Crumbs (page 34)

¾ cup chicken stock

Make the béchamel sauce and set aside.

Preheat the oven to 350 degrees F.

In a large stockpot of boiling salted water, cook the lobsters for 10 minutes. Then drain the lobsters and allow to cool.

In a large sauté pan, heat the olive oil, add the chopped garlic, and cook until the garlic is brown. Now add the celery and onion, cooking until the onion is translucent. Add the thyme, butter, and mushrooms; sauté over medium-low heat for 5 minutes, or until the mushrooms are tender. Remove from the heat and set aside.

To prepare a lobster, remove the claws, tail, and head. Discard the head. With a pair of scissors, remove the shell under the tail, keeping the outer, harder shell intact. This outer shell is going to be your cup to hold the meat. With a mallet or cracker, remove all the meat, and chop into a large dice. Do this with all the lobsters. Place the pan with the vegetable mixture over medium heat. Add the lobster meat, Parmigiano Reggiano, and béchamel sauce, and mix well. Scoop an equal amount of the lobster mixture into each lobster tail. Top with the grated cheddar cheese and toasted bread crumbs, and place in a baking or lasagna pan. Place the remaining butter and chicken stock on the bottom of the pan. Bake in the oven for 10 to 15 minutes, or until the bread crumbs have browned and the sauce is bubbling. Serve immediately.

HEARTY SEA BASS

SERVES 4

Usually, white-fish dishes are light. The thing I like about this one is that it's earthier than, say, a piece of fish with lemon butter. Beans and basil are a no-brainer, and adding them to a good piece of sea bass makes for a great combination. **If you can't find sea bass, halibut would work here, too.**

Four 8-ounce fillets of Chilean sea bass (center cut), skin and bones removed

½ teaspoon kosher salt

½ teaspoon freshly ground black pepper

½ teaspoon granulated garlic

All-purpose flour, for dredging

¼ cup vegetable oil

2 tablespoons extra-virgin olive oil

6 garlic cloves, smashed

12 Littleneck clams, washed

2 tablespoons Pinot Grigio

6 ounces San Marzano whole tomatoes, hand-crushed

3 fresh basil leaves

¼ cup canned or cooked white kidney beans, drained

1 tablespoon butter

2 cups fresh spinach, packed

Season the sea bass with half the salt, half the pepper, and half the granulated garlic, and dredge in flour. In a large sauté pan, heat the vegetable oil until hot but not smoking. Sear the fillets on both sides until they are brown. Remove the fish from the pan, and set aside.

Discard the vegetable oil, and replace it with the olive oil. Add the smashed garlic, and cook until it is brown. Next, add the clams, deglaze the pan with wine, and add the San Marzano tomatoes, basil, and beans. Season the sauce with the remaining salt, pepper, and granulated garlic, then return the fish to the pan. Cover, and cook on medium-high heat for 8 to 10 minutes (the fish should be firm), adding the butter and spinach a minute before serving. Place each piece of fish on a plate, pour sauce on top, and serve.

SHORT RIBS

SERVES 4

You have to cook short ribs in the oven until the meat falls off the bone. Sometimes at the restaurant we'll get rid of the bone, shred the meat a little, and put it back into the juices from the roasting pan before tossing it all with pappardelle. Or we'll leave the meat on the bone and serve it with polenta. Either way, it's great.

Four 16-ounce bone-in short ribs

1 tablespoon kosher salt, plus more for sauce

1 tablespoon freshly ground black pepper, plus more for sauce

1 tablespoon granulated garlic, plus more for sauce

¼ cup vegetable oil

1 cup extra-virgin olive oil

¼ cup whole garlic, minced

1 cup ¼-inch dice celery

1 cup ¼-inch dice carrot

1 cup ¼-inch dice yellow onion

1 cup Chianti

1½ cups chicken stock

2 cups demi-glace (reduced veal stock)

2 dried bay leaves

Two 28-ounce cans San Marzano whole tomatoes, hand-crushed

1 cup chopped fresh Italian parsley

2 cups grated Parmigiano Reggiano, plus more for serving

Preheat the oven to 400 degrees F. Evenly season the short ribs with the salt, pepper, and granulated garlic. Heat a large metal roasting pan on the stovetop over high heat with vegetable oil. Sear the ribs, allowing them to brown on all sides; then remove from the pan and set aside.

Remove the vegetable oil, and replace it with the olive oil. Add the minced garlic and allow it to brown, then add the celery, carrot, and onion, and cook until the onion is translucent. Deglaze the pan with the Chianti; then add the chicken stock, demi-glace, bay leaves, San Marzano tomatoes, and ribs; season the sauce with salt, pepper, and granulated garlic, and bring to a boil.

Place the whole pan, covered, in the oven, and cook for 2½ hours, or until the meat starts to fall off the bone. Remember to stir the sauce occasionally, to prevent burning on the bottom. Remove from the oven, and skim any excess fat from the gravy. If you like, remove the bones from the short ribs. Add the parsley and Parmigiano Reggiano, and simmer on the stovetop for 15 minutes.

Place each short rib on a plate, top with gravy, garnish with freshly grated Parmigiano Reggiano, and serve.

SHRIMP SCAMPI

SERVES 4

About 20 years ago, basketball legend Wilt Chamberlain came into my Fort Lauderdale restaurant and wanted shrimp scampi. It wasn't on the menu, but the big guy wasn't going to take no for an answer. I went back into the kitchen and whipped this up. **Wilt flipped, and it stayed on the menu.** Now it's one of our most popular items.

4 jumbo shrimp, shells on
    but deveined

Pinch of kosher salt

Pinch of freshly ground black pepper

Pinch of granulated garlic

¼ **cup extra-virgin olive oil**

6 **garlic cloves, smashed**

¼ **cup Pinot Grigio**

1½ **cups Clam Stock (recipe follows)**

2 **ounces cherry tomatoes**

2 **ounces green peas**

4 **tablespoons salted butter, coated**
    with all-purpose flour

Homemade Toasted Bread Crumbs
    (page 34)

½ **teaspoon finely chopped fresh**
    Italian parsley

Season the shrimp with the salt, pepper, and granulated garlic. Heat a large sauté pan with the olive oil, and sear the shrimp for 1 minute on each side. Add the garlic, and cook until golden brown. Deglaze the pan with the wine, cooking until it has reduced to almost nothing. Then add the clam stock, cherry tomatoes, and green peas. Next, add the butter dredged in flour to the sauce. Cover, and cook for 5 to 7 minutes, until the sauce becomes thick and the shrimp are fully cooked. Divide among four plates, garnish with toasted bread crumbs and fresh parsley, and serve.

CLAM STOCK

MAKES 1 QUART

2 **tablespoons extra-virgin olive oil**

¼ **cup garlic cloves, smashed**

20 **chowder clams, soaked and**
    rinsed clean

¼ **cup Pinot Grigio**

2 **cups water**

We use quahog clams for our stock; you can also use Littlenecks or cherrystones. We use enough of the stock so we use it fresh, but you can also freeze it. These guys are loaded with flavor. We save the shells and stuff them with crabmeat (see Clams Martorano on page 102).

In a large pot over medium-high heat, heat the olive oil and brown the garlic. Next, add the clams, and cook for 5 minutes. Then add the wine, allow the alcohol to cook off for 2 minutes, add the water, and cover. Once the clams have opened, strain the stock into a container and discard the clams.

FRESH TUNA WITH WHOLE-WHEAT SPAGHETTI

SERVES 4

This is one of those rare things that I make better than my mom. She used canned tuna, which was fine—but fresh is much, much better. I use whole-wheat pasta for this dish because it's a little better for you, but you can use regular pasta.

Sea salt, for pasta water

1 pound whole-wheat spaghetti

¼ cup extra-virgin olive oil

5 garlic cloves, smashed

8 salt-packed capers

6 taggiasca olives, pitted (or substitute French Niçoise or Italian Gaeta olives)

2 anchovy fillets, whole

8 ounces fresh big-eye Hawaiian tuna, cut into ½-inch cubes

8 ounces whole San Marzano tomatoes, hand-crushed

2 teaspoons kosher salt

2 teaspoons freshly ground black pepper

2 teaspoons dried oregano

2 fresh basil leaves, torn

Bring salted water to a boil, and cook the spaghetti until al dente, 9 to 10 minutes.

Meanwhile, pour the olive oil into a large hot sauté pan, add the garlic, and cook until it is brown. Now add the capers, olives, anchovies, and tuna, and cook for 2 minutes. Then, add the San Marzano tomatoes, season with the salt, pepper, and oregano, and cook for 3 minutes.

Strain the pasta through a colander, toss it into the sauce, and add the freshly torn basil. Divide the pasta and sauce among four plates, and serve.

VEAL SINATRA

SERVES 4

I'm a huge Frank Sinatra fan. To me, he was like a pope. I love all of his movies and music so much that **I even have a Sinatra tattoo.** I created this dish in his honor many years ago, and everything about it is over the top, the best—just like the man himself. The funny thing is, he probably wouldn't have liked this dish. Friends of his have told me that a typical dinner for Sinatra was pretty simple, like a pasta.

2 South African lobster tails

Kosher salt and freshly ground black pepper to taste

Granulated garlic to taste

¼ cup butter

4 ounces button mushrooms, sliced ⅛ inch thick

¼ cup dry Marsala wine

1 cup heavy cream

¼ cup vegetable oil

Four 3-ounce slices veal tenderloin, pounded thin

All-purpose flour, for dredging

On a cutting board, slice the lobster tails in half lengthwise, and season with salt, pepper, and granulated garlic. Melt the butter in a sauté pan over medium heat, and add the mushrooms and lobster. Sauté until the mushrooms are golden brown and the lobster shell is bright red.

Next, remove the pan from the heat and deglaze it with the Marsala wine. Add the heavy cream, and bring the pan to a simmer.

In a separate pan, heat the vegetable oil until hot but not smoking. Season the pounded veal cutlets on both sides with salt, pepper, and granulated garlic. Dredge both sides of the veal with flour, and add the slices to the hot pan. Cook, turning once, until golden brown on both sides. Remove the veal and let the slices drain on paper towels, then add the cooked veal to the cream sauce. Continue cooking to reduce the sauce until it becomes creamy and coats the back of a spoon.

To serve, put a slice of the veal on each plate, and top with a piece of lobster tail and Sinatra sauce.

VEAL PICCATA

SERVES 4

Most recipes for veal piccata make it seem as simple as buying a piece of veal and squeezing a lemon. Yeah, you can do that. But **if you want to take this dish to the next level, use veal stock** and, if you can find one, a Meyer lemon, which has the sweeter taste of an orange and a lemon combined.

¼ cup vegetable oil

Four 3-ounce slices veal tenderloin, pounded thin

¼ teaspoon kosher salt

¼ teaspoon freshly ground black pepper

¼ teaspoon granulated garlic

All-purpose flour, for dredging

LEMON BUTTER SAUCE

2 tablespoons Pinot Grigio

¾ cup chicken stock

Juice of ½ lemon

1 tablespoon butter, coated with all-purpose flour

1 tablespoon roughly chopped fresh Italian parsley

1 tablespoon salt-packed capers

In a large sauté pan, heat the vegetable oil. Season the veal with the salt, pepper, and granulated garlic, and then lightly flour both sides of veal. Sear the veal in the hot oil, allowing it to brown on both sides. Then remove it from pan and set aside.

Add the wine to a separate hot pan, and allow the alcohol to burn off. Then add the chicken stock, lemon juice, and butter coated with flour. Simmer the sauce until it becomes thick and coats the back of a spoon. Add the veal to the pan, and coat with sauce. Place each piece of veal on a plate, top with the sauce, and garnish with parsley and capers.

YO CUZ!

FRESH START

I'M A HANDS-ON GUY. No matter what I do, I like to have a measure of control over the process. I want things done right, and I want them done my way. I guess that makes me a perfectionist. My father was a stubborn guy. Add those two things together and you have a recipe for disaster.

After months of trying to convince him that he and I could make my uncle Raymond's bar into a successful bar *and* restaurant, I thought I'd finally won him over when we packed Anton's with customers for a dinner-and-a-movie night. The *Godfather* night was a hit, but I knew it was just a first step and realized that we were going to need to spend money to make money. My father liked the first part of that equation—the hit part—but he wasn't willing to relinquish control or open his wallet to build on what we'd accomplished. After a failed follow-up effort, I abandoned the idea of our working together and struck out on my own.

Dream big; it's free.

I started a new business, Steve's Italian Kitchen, but it really wasn't much of a kitchen at all. It was my one-bedroom apartment—where I kept a meat slicer on the counter and fresh cold cuts in the refrigerator. Outside, on the street, there was no room for parking, and I often left my car running and double-parked while I unloaded the groceries for making sandwiches.

During the mornings, I'd draw fliers by hand: "Steve's Italian Kitchen— the Best Hoagies in Philly." For the next three hours, I'd go to different neighborhoods, passing them out to people on the street and putting them on cars and in mailboxes. Then I'd go home and wait for the phone to ring. It never did, and I'd leave for the night to spin records, disappointed. But I fought through the discouragement and did it all again the next day.

With my father's blessing, I even began listing Anton's address on the fliers, in hopes of legitimizing what I was doing. But after a month of hard work, I was still throwing good food in the trash and flushing money down the toilet. I never stopped believing in myself, though.

Three months into my venture, the phone finally rang. It was 8:00 p.m. I was just about to call it quits for the day and go out to work at the clubs.

"I want two Italian hoagies," said the lady on the other end of the line.

I sliced the lunch meat and tomatoes, chopped the lettuce and onions, made the hoagies, and delivered them. The bill came to $7.80, and the lady gave me a $2.20 tip. My first sale. I was bursting with pride. This was it, I thought, my big break—on my own. What a feeling. It was like getting a girl's number.

The next morning, I got up early to prepare for the day ahead. The phone, I figured, would be ringing off the hook. I went out into the street, handed out my fliers, and hustled home to take the orders. Plus, I wanted to be home when my first customer called to tell me how great those sandwiches were.

The phone never rang.

It got late, and again I wrapped up the lunch meat, cleaned the slicer, and got ready for the club. At 8:00 p.m., the phone rang. It was my first customer—Mrs. Right, I called her, because she knew I made the right hoagie for her.

"I want two more hoagies," said the lady. "Those first two were delicious."

It was a small step, but I wasn't going to look back. Repeat business—that was going to be the start of my success.

By the end of that first year, 1983, my sandwich business had picked up considerably. People were starting to take notice—especially my landlord. He made a big fuss and threatened to call the cops, so I sneaked my food and equipment onto a borrowed truck and headed to my mother's basement on Newkirk Street.

ABOVE *My mother's house on Newkirk Street: "the basement where it all started"*

She was thrilled, and I didn't have to pay for rent, gas, electric, or a phone. My mother was always around to answer the phone to take orders, and even helped wash pots and pans. We added spaghetti and meatballs, chicken-cutlet-and-broccoli-rabe sandwiches, veal-parm sandwiches, homemade soups, and spaghetti with crabs on Friday.

It ended up being one of my best business moves.

EVEN THOUGH BUSINESS WAS GREAT during that time period, my personal life was stressful. I was engaged to Debbie, an Italian girl from Northeast Philly. We had met in the one of the clubs, and I was excited to start a new life, but it felt like my old one was crumbling around me.

In 1983, my cousin Georgie Martorano was convicted and sentenced to life without parole for running a $75-million-a-year drug ring. (He's been in prison for more than thirty years, becoming the longest-serving nonviolent offender in a federal prison in U.S. history. I think he's done his time and earned a pardon. He needs to come home.) A few months later, in 1984, things went from bad to worse when Uncle Raymond was tried, convicted, and sentenced to life in prison as well for the murder of a union boss.

Then, two weeks before my wedding, the worst thing imaginable happened. One morning I woke to my mother's screaming to find that my father had died of a massive heart attack. She found him on the floor in front of the parlor TV. It wasn't unusual for him to fall asleep like that (he couldn't get comfortable on a bed), but this time he didn't wake up. He was fifty-four.

At one point, I was left alone in the parlor with my father's body. I called my uncles, then the undertaker. I sat and waited by myself, staring at the body. There were a lot of things that I said to him over the years that I shouldn't have. So I leaned over, kissed him, and told him that I was sorry and I loved him.

When the undertaker arrived, I helped put my father in a bag and I zipped it shut. Because my father was so large, I had to help carry him to the hearse. I gave the undertaker some money and left to buy my father a suit. I decided that Joe Martorano was finally going to get something new, and I was paying for it.

The authorities released Uncle Raymond for the memorial service. Before he arrived, cops were posted on the corners in front of the funeral

ABOVE *At Coleman Federal Penitentiary visiting my cousin Georgie*

home. Television crews set up on the street, and one of their helicopters hovered in the air above. Raymond arrived at the door. His feet and hands were shackled, and he was escorted by two officers. I was furious with the cops, and I started making a scene, calling them motherfuckers.

"I'm not going to embarrass my nephew and his family like this," said Uncle Raymond before entering the funeral home. "Take me back."

A week after we buried my father, Uncle John, one of my father's other brothers, called me into his office. He wanted to talk about my working for Uncle Raymond.

I swallowed hard and prayed to the Blessed Mother to help me make good decisions.

"What? Loading trucks? Fixing jukeboxes? No, no, no—forget about that."

"You gotta do the right thing," he said. "You gotta take up for your father. It's time to come with us."

All I could think of was the $166 a week my father was making when he died. I wasn't going to end up like my father; my uncle's offer was unacceptable. I had a lot of anger in me. So I swallowed hard and prayed to the Blessed Mother to help me make good decisions.

IN THE DAYS LEADING UP TO MY WEDDING, my mother began sorting through my father's belongings. She handed me a worn, tiny piece of paper that had been carefully folded and refolded. On the paper were a lot of numbers and initials written in what looked to be code—men who owed my father money. Guys like my father never had a bank account. All he owned was either in his pocket or on the street.

We spent all of my father's insurance money on the funeral. It was my responsibility to go and collect the money that was owed my family. Thousands of dollars on the street were due. My father always taught me that you didn't want the guy to pay his loan off, you wanted the juice on the loan—no more loan, no more juice coming. On the street, the custom was that if the loan shark lent you money and then died, the debt was squashed. But we needed the money. That tradition wasn't going to work for me.

One by one, I tracked down the men over the course of the next few days.

"Oh, I just paid him last month," said one guy.

"Your dad said we were even, kid," said another.

"He said I didn't owe him the whole thing," said a third asshole.

By the time I found another man and he gave me the same story as the others, I was angry and lost control. This one was in a bar. I threw the motherfucker against the wall and put my hands around his neck. His eyes bulged, and he rifled through his pockets for his wallet.

"Just take it," he said. "Take it all."

It wasn't even half of what he owed, but I crumpled the bills, put them in my pocket, and spit in his face.

"That's my father's money," I said. "Now it's mine. Pay me the rest tomorrow, or I'll finish what I started."

SHORTLY AFTER DEBBIE AND I WERE MARRIED—just a few months after my father had passed—we moved into a townhouse in Northeast Philadelphia. Given all that had recently happened, it was probably best to leave the neighborhood for a while and start fresh. But, unlike South Philly, this neighborhood had a large Jewish population and wasn't known for its Italian food. Still, there were a number of restaurants in the area; even though none of them was worth a shit, they appeared to have a good, if mostly older, clientele.

One night, Debbie and I tried an Italian place where people were lined up outside, waiting to get in. I ordered some stuffed mushrooms. They were spoiled, and the rest of the food was just as bad.

I picked at my plate and looked at the line outside.

"If this is the best they've got, and I opened here, we'd be millionaires," I said.

What I didn't know at the time was that most of their clientele wanted soup, salad, entrée, and dessert—for $6.99. At this point in my life, I wasn't going to get out of bed for $6.99.

I closed down the business in my mother's basement, opened a take-out place, and struggled again. Seemed like, no matter what I did, nothing came easy. I made Debbie quit her job to work with me. These people here in the Northeast weren't used to Italian comfort food, didn't really understand what I was trying to do, and my sandwiches weren't cheap. Quality is never cheap.

I needed a way to make the business work.

With the summer approaching, I decided to sell Italian water ice—

ABOVE *My first free-standing place*

ABOVE *My first takeout business after the basement*

a big business in Philly, but only in the summer. A friend of mine owned John's Water Ice in South Philly, and was willing to help me out. We were going to buy the product from John's—a fifty-minute round-trip—and sell it at our place.

The night before we were going to start selling the water ice, Debbie woke up in the middle of the night with the idea of making our own water ice.

We purchased a used water-ice machine and experimented over the next few days. Within a month, we had the best water ice in Northeast Philly, with lines around the corner. Customers requested water ice more than other food, especially gelati (layers of water ice, gelato, and more water ice). We saved $100,000 in one season. I had big plans.

"Let's spend it," I said in January 1987, "and open a restaurant. We'll call it Steve's Italian Kitchen—a nice sit-down place, with takeout and a little window on the side of the building to sell water ice."

I purchased a building that was for sale around the corner from my takeout place. But as soon as we opened, the city closed the street in front of my place for repairs, and it almost killed us. I was located in the middle of a street that was ripped up—you couldn't drive up or down the street. This was before the Internet, and I needed parking and regular traffic so people could actually discover us.

Those first couple of months, especially the winter ones, were tough, and we just barely made it. Lots of days, I'd sit in front of the takeout window and stare out into the cold, gray street. I got down on my knees and prayed a lot, but, most important, I got off my ass and talked up the restaurant around the neighborhood. I'd walk up and down the sidewalks of that ripped-up street and talk to whoever would listen—whether I was in front of a funeral home or a pet store, it didn't matter.

Eventually, people who loved good food found us, and things were good. I had people dressed in suits and ties waiting in line for a table—class all the way. We decided to remodel, make the joint into something fancier, and change the name to Steve's Ristorante. We changed the menu

ABOVE *My first takeout business after the basement*

and prices to give the place a more upscale feel. But nobody, including me, knew what a fucking *ristorante* should be. Big mistake. No one came. They wanted my old-school food, but I was trying something fancier. With every move I made, I was getting further and further from the things I knew best. A lesson I learned: never

A lesson I learned: never forget who you are or where you come from.

forget who you are or where you come from. I wasn't a chef; I was a neighborhood cook.

WHEN THE FIRST GULF WAR HIT, my business went into the toilet. Oil prices had soared, and the economy tanked. What was worse, though, was that I'd done most of the damage myself. I never had anyone to teach me the business, so much of what I was doing was trial and error. And there were lots of errors. But I wasn't going to cut corners. My mother would scream at me for using quality stuff, but that was the only way I knew.

"You're going to go broke," she'd cry. "What do your customers know about good olive oil? Give them the cheaper stuff. They won't know the difference. Spending all this money—you're like a crazy person."

I tried digging myself out of the hole, but only made a bigger one by throwing money and credit cards at the problem. In June 1991, we closed and we said were remodeling. But that was bullshit. To keep money coming in, I sold water ice again—25 and 50 cents a scoop—from the tiny corner of a huge building that was largely empty.

I thought about my father and Anton's. How was selling water ice for quarters any different from pouring shots and beers for the same? But I wasn't going to give up, because I knew I wasn't a failure—I just had a failed restaurant on my hands. There's really something to that old saying, "Location, location, location."

IN 1992, I BEGAN TOYING WITH THE IDEA of moving south—way past South Philly, to Florida. I figured maybe that was the location that would work for me.

Debbie and I made arrangements to visit friends in the Fort Lauderdale area, but before we left, I put in a call to Raymond Abruzzi, an old family friend. Abruzzi—who played for the New York Jets and years earlier had opened the Upper East Side bar Bachelors III in New York with his old teammate Joe Namath—had moved to Fort Lauderdale and opened another Bachelors III. I hoped he'd be willing to offer some advice about how to start a new venture in Florida.

For the most part, the trip was nice but largely uneventful. During the days, we did tourist-type things; at night, I'd drive around the area, scouting vacant properties. But by sunset, the entire community seemed to be already in bed. It appeared to be a great place to raise a family, which was a consideration—by then, Debbie and I had two small boys, Joey and Steven—but Fort Lauderdale offered little in the way of nightlife. I was disappointed and frustrated. Debbie and my kids were depending on me, and I felt I was letting everyone down. Before we left for the airport to return to Philly, I put in another call to Ray and explained the situation.

I had a good feeling about my new little place in Fort Lauderdale. I believed—I knew—it was going to be a success.

"Cuz, there's nothing for me here. These people are asleep by nine o'clock. I'm going back to Philly to do what I got to do." At that point, I didn't even know what that might mean.

"Stop being such a jerk-off," Abruzzi said. "Get that South Philly mentality out of your head."

Ray told me about a property across from his condo. I was skeptical, but, out of respect for Ray, decided to swing by and take a look before we left for Philly. On the way to the airport, we stopped by the strip mall on Oakland Park Boulevard. I looked in the window. It was small—eight hundred square feet or so—but I fell in love. On the spot, I decided to buy the place.

When we got back to Philly, I worked the phones and made the deals. I put a down payment on the restaurant and a home, then bought equipment and supplies.

So, with my pockets practically empty, I headed to Fort Lauderdale. When everything was said and done, I only had $40 to my name. Forty dollars wasn't going to go far. I wasn't stupid—crazy, maybe. Anyway, my balls were big, and I didn't worry about failing. More important, I still believed in myself.

I knew 90 percent of restaurants failed within a year of opening their doors, and Oakland Park Boulevard in Fort Lauderdale wasn't fucking Broad Street in South Philly. There was no foot traffic, unless you counted the hookers, or the bums who would pass out in the parking lot on their way to the liquor store down the street. A drugstore anchored one corner of the shopping center, but, aside from a dry cleaner's and my restaurant, the rest of the stores were vacant.

Inside, the walls were painted in pastels–pinks and blues that made me want to throw up. Eight small tables with pink plastic tablecloths were scattered about, and there was only one fridge, one stove, and one pizza oven–and I didn't even make pizza at that time.

Still, I had a good feeling about my new little place in Fort Lauderdale. I believed–I knew–it was going to be a success. But it needed a great name. I thought of my father and uncle and everything our family had been through, and decided that this new restaurant should carry the Martorano name.

And with that, Cafe Martorano was born.

Next, we needed some rules. My rules. I was the boss and was going to carry this place on my shoulders, if that's what it needed to be great. That pink-and-blue bullshit had to go. What–was Cinderella going to cook here? I was a black-and-white kinda guy, so we painted the walls, and put the pink tablecloths in the Dumpster, where they belonged. I didn't give a fuck if those were Florida colors or not; I was from South Philly.

I decided that because of our limited resources, I was obviously going to do all of the cooking; Debbie would wait tables, my mother could play hostess, and I had hired a Cuban kid to wash dishes. There weren't going to be any substitutions or special orders, either. We couldn't afford to put up with that kind of crap, so I let people know where I stood, right on the bottom of the menu, in black and white: NO SUBSTITUTIONS. DON'T BREAK BALLS. And, most important, I was going to stay true to myself. This wasn't going to be a *ristorante*–whatever the fuck that was. I'd made that mistake before. Not this time. Cafe Martorano was going to be all me– from the heart. I was going to serve the dishes I grew up with and cook like Frank Sinatra sang–my way.

ABOVE *The original Cafe Martorano– 800 square feet–in Fort Lauderdale*

YO CUZ!

DESSERTS AND DRINKS

CANNOLI CREAM

TO FILL 6 CANNOLI SHELLS

We don't make **cannoli shells** in any of my restaurants; we buy them. **You can find them in a lot of good markets, specialty stores, and Italian bakeries.** Buy and freeze them; when you have last-minute company or need to make a great dessert in a pinch, you're halfway done.

3 cups ricotta

1¼ cups confectioners' sugar

¼ teaspoon ground cinnamon

¼ cup chocolate chips

1 teaspoon vanilla extract

6 large cannoli shells

Put the ricotta in a bowl and, whisking with a wire whisk, add the confectioners' sugar slowly, mixing until well incorporated. Add all the other ingredients, and mix until well blended. Place the mixture in a piping bag, and fill in your cannoli shells on both ends.

MARSHA'S RED VELVET CAKE

SERVES 8 TO 12

Marsha Daley, my girlfriend, loves to bake. She's really talented. Still, I asked her to perfect this recipe. **It took about four months of trial and error.** Sometimes it was a little too moist, sometimes a little too dry. "Nope, not there yet," I'd tell her. I knew she had it just right when I couldn't stop eating it. **Nothing's better than this cake and a glass of ice-cold milk.**

2 cups all-purpose flour

1 teaspoon baking soda

1 teaspoon baking powder

1 teaspoon salt

2 tablespoons unsweetened cocoa powder

2 cups granulated sugar

½ cup vegetable oil

½ cup of melted unsalted butter

2 large eggs

1 cup buttermilk

2 teaspoons vanilla extract

2 teaspoons red food coloring

1 teaspoon distilled white vinegar

½ cup brewed black coffee

2 tablespoons unsalted butter

All-purpose flour, for dusting the pans

CREAM-CHEESE ICING

3 pounds cream cheese, cut into small cubes, at room temperature

1 pound unsalted butter, cut into small pieces, softened

2 pounds confectioners' sugar

Preheat the oven to 325 degrees F. In a medium bowl, mix the flour, baking soda, baking powder, salt, and cocoa powder with a wire whisk. In a separate bowl, mix the granulated sugar, vegetable oil, and melted butter. In another bowl, combine the eggs, buttermilk, vanilla, food coloring, vinegar, and coffee until they are well blended. Make a well in the middle of the dry ingredients. Slowly add the wet ingredients to the well, and mix until the mixture is just combined. Generously grease and flour three 6-inch baking pans, and pour an equal amount of batter into each pan. Bake in the center of the oven for 30 to 40 minutes, or until a toothpick inserted in the center comes out clean.

TO MAKE THE CREAM-CHEESE ICING In a stand mixer, or using a handheld egg beater, mix the cream cheese until smooth. With the mixer at medium speed, slowly add the butter to the cream cheese, allowing the butter to dissolve into the cream cheese before adding more. Scrape down the sides of the bowl to ensure that everything is distributed evenly. When the butter is all whipped into the cream cheese, slowly add the sugar. When all the sugar is well incorporated, turn the mixer to high speed, and whip until smooth.

When the cakes are cool to the touch, remove them from the pans and place on flat plates. Warm a metal spatula in hot water, and evenly spread the cream-cheese icing on the top of one cake. Put another cake on top, and repeat the process. Finally, add the third layer, and cover the top and sides of the cake with icing. Place in the refrigerator for at least 20 minutes before cutting.

BROWNIES

SERVES 6

This might look like a basic dessert, but, believe it or not, my chefs, Walter Pytel and Dave Algor, spent a week or so getting this one just right. **It was worth all of the work.** There's nothing better than one of these **hot brownies with a scoop or two of vanilla ice cream.**

2 cups semi-sweet chocolate chips, plus ½ cup for topping

6 tablespoons salted butter, plus 2 tablespoons for the pan

3½ cups sugar

6 large eggs

2¼ cups all-purpose flour, sifted, plus 2 tablespoons for the pan

Preheat the oven to 350 degrees F. Boil water in a medium saucepan, and turn the heat down to medium-low. Place a metal bowl on top of this pot to create a double boiler. Place the chocolate and butter in the bowl, and allow them to melt, stirring together. Meanwhile, put the sugar and eggs in another bowl, and beat well. Once the chocolate and butter are melted, slowly add the mixture to the eggs and sugar. When everything is blended, add the sifted flour to the mixture, and mix until incorporated.

Thoroughly grease and flour a lasagna pan, add the batter, and top with chocolate chips. Bake in the oven for 30 minutes. Cut the brownies with a knife into six servings, and remove each brownie with a metal spatula. Place the brownies on plates, and serve with your favorite vanilla ice cream.

PEANUT BUTTER CAKE WITH PEANUT BUTTER ZABAGLIONE

SERVES 6

My chef Walter Pytel created this dessert. **I love peanut butter, but out of the jar**—not in my food. When I tried this creation, I changed my mind.

¼ cup salted butter, plus more
    for greasing pans

1 cup all-purpose flour, sifted, plus
    more for coating pans

3½ ounces semisweet chocolate chips

3 eggs

¾ cup sugar

Pinch of kosher salt

2 tablespoons creamy peanut butter

ZABAGLIONE

6 egg yolks

½ cup granulated sugar

1 tablespoon creamy peanut butter

4 cups heavy cream

1 teaspoon vanilla extract

¾ cup confectioners' sugar

Chocolate syrup, for garnish

ABOVE *Chef Walter Pytel*

Preheat the oven to 325 degrees F. Grease two 6-inch cake pans with butter, dust with flour, and set aside. Put the butter and chocolate chips in a metal bowl, set it over a pot of simmering water, and allow to melt. In a separate bowl, beat the eggs and granulated sugar together until well blended. When the chocolate and butter have melted, add 2 tablespoons of creamy peanut butter, and mix well. While mixing vigorously, slowly add the egg mixture to the chocolate mixture. Then pour the whole thing into the sifted flour, add the salt, and mix until it's well blended. Pour the batter into the cake pans, and place on a rack in the center of the oven. Cook for 20 minutes, or until a toothpick inserted in the center comes out dry. Allow the cake to cool, remove the layers from the pans, and place them on a plate.

TO MAKE THE ZABAGLIONE Beat the egg yolks and granulated sugar together in a metal bowl, and place over a pot of simmering water. Mix continuously with a whisk, beating the eggs and sugar together. Be sure the pan is over no more than medium heat, so the eggs don't scramble. Keep stirring until the eggs double in size and the mixture becomes thick. At this point, add the peanut butter and remove from the heat. Next, with an egg beater, mix together the heavy cream, vanilla, and confectioners' sugar, and beat until the cream comes to a firm peak. Take a third of the heavy cream and fold it into the peanut-butter mixture. Mix gently until all the cream is absorbed. Then take another third and gently fold it into the mixture. Repeat until all the cream is folded in.

Place one cake layer down on a plate, scoop a third of the zabaglione on top of it, and spread evenly. Now top with the other cake, and completely cover the top and sides of the cake with the rest of the zabaglione. Allow to sit in the refrigerator for at least 20 minutes. Decorate the top of the cake with some chocolate syrup, and enjoy.

ZABAGLIONE WITH BERRIES

SERVES 6

Since there's no baking involved, you can whip up this **great Sicilian dessert** in no time.

½ cup sweet Marsala

6 egg yolks

½ cup granulated sugar

4 cups heavy cream

1 teaspoon vanilla extract

¾ cup confectioners' sugar

1 pint strawberries

1 pint blueberries

1 pint raspberries

1 pint blackberries

2 tablespoons fresh mint leaves, torn

In a small pan, bring the Marsala to a boil—be careful, it might flame up. In a metal bowl, mix together the egg yolks and granulated sugar, and place the bowl over a pot of simmering water. Mixing continuously with a whisk, beat the eggs and sugar, and add the hot Marsala. Be sure the pan is over no more than medium heat, so the eggs don't scramble. Keep stirring until the eggs double in size and the mixture becomes thick. At this point, remove from the heat. Next, with an egg beater, beat together the heavy cream, vanilla, and confectioners' sugar, until the cream comes to a firm peak. Take a third of the heavy cream and fold it into egg-and-Marsala mixture. Mix gently until all the cream is absorbed. Then take another third and gently fold that into the mixture. Repeat until all the cream is folded together.

Wash all the berries, and towel-dry. Remove the stems from the strawberries and cut them into quarters. Place all the berries in a bowl, and mix together; toss in the zabaglione mixture, and gently coat the berries. Divide among six plates, and serve garnished with freshly torn mint.

ANGEL

MAKES 1 COCKTAIL

2 lime wedges

1 ounce Herradura Añejo tequila

¼ ounce Cointreau Noir liqueur

¼ ounce Pêche de Vigne peach liqueur

1 ounce margarita mix

1 ounce apricot nectar

GARNISH sugar for glass rim, lime wedge

Fill a glass with ice, and squeeze 2 lime wedges over the ice into the glass. Pour in the liquors, margarita mix, and nectar, and mix over the ice in the glass. Pour the contents into a tall shaking tin. Cap the tin with the short shaker, and give a vigorous short shake. Dip the rim of a highball or tall glass with sugar, fill with ice, and pour the cocktail into it. Place a lime wedge on the rim of the glass.

BLACK BEAUTY MARTINI

MAKES 1 COCKTAIL

1½ ounces Absolut Berri Açai vodka

½ ounce Frangelico

Juice of 1 lemon wedge

4 fresh blackberries

GARNISH lemon twist

Combine all the ingredients except the garnish in a large shaking tin. Muddle the blackberries. Add 10 to 12 ounces ice, and shake vigorously twelve to fourteen times. Pour into a chilled martini glass. Garnish the rim of the glass with a thin lemon twist.

COSMO BIANCO

MAKES 1 COCKTAIL

1¼ ounces Imperia vodka

¾ ounce Cointreau liqueur

1 ounce white cranberry juice

GARNISH 3 fresh red cranberries

Combine all of the ingredients except the garnish in a large shaking tin. Add 10 to 12 ounces ice. Shake vigorously twelve to fourteen times. Strain the cocktail into a martini glass. Garnish the drink with 3 floating fresh cranberries.

CRYSTAL GRAPE MARTINI

MAKES 1 COCKTAIL

¾ ounce Absolut Pears vodka

¾ ounce St. Germain liqueur

5 small grapes, red or green

2 ounces Prosecco

GARNISH 3 grapes

Combine the first three ingredients in a large shaking tin. Muddle the grapes. Add 10 to 12 ounces ice, and shake vigorously twelve to fourteen times. Pour into a chilled martini glass. Top the cocktail with the Prosecco, and garnish with the grapes.

HARVEST PEACH MARTINI

MAKES 1 COCKTAIL

1¼ ounces American Harvest
 Organic vodka

¾ ounce Pêche de Vigne peach
 liqueur

1 ounce The Perfect White Peach
 Purée

1 ounce freshly squeezed orange
 juice

GARNISH crescent slice of orange,
 strawberry

Combine all of the ingredients except the garnish in a large shaking tin, with 10 ounces ice. Shake twelve to fourteen times, then strain into a martini glass. Float the orange crescent slice and the strawberry atop the cocktail.

METROPOLITAN MARTINI

MAKES 1 COCKTAIL

1 ounce American Harvest Organic
    vodka

½ ounce Domaine de Canton ginger
    liqueur

½ ounce Bärenjäger Honey Liqueur

1 ounce sour mix

½ ounce freshly squeezed grapefruit
    juice

3 dashes Angostura Bitters

GARNISH lemon twist

Combine all of the ingredients except the garnish in a large shaking tin. Add 10 to 12 ounces ice, then shake vigorously twelve to fourteen times and pour into a chilled martini glass. Garnish with the lemon twist.

SICILIAN MULE

MAKES 1 COCKTAIL

2 lime wedges

2 ounces vodka

6 ounces ginger beer

GARNISH lime wedge

Place 16 ounces ice in a copper mug. Squeeze 2 lime wedges over the ice, then add the vodka. Fill with the ginger beer. Garnish with a lime wedge.

SIMPLY RED MARTINI

MAKES 1 COCKTAIL

2 ounces Ketel One vodka

1 ounce simple syrup

4 strawberries

2 fresh basil leaves

GARNISH strawberry-and-basil flag
    (see procedure)

Combine all of the ingredients except the garnish in a large shaking tin. Muddle the ingredients together five or six times. Add 10 ounces ice, and shake twelve to fourteen times. Strain into a martini glass. Poke a nice piece of basil leaf through a walnut-sized strawberry, then hang it on the rim of the glass.

TWISTED BERRY COCKTAIL

MAKES 1 COCKTAIL

¾ ounce Penacho Azteca Añejo
    tequila

¾ ounce Veev Açai Spirit liqueur

¾ ounce organic blue-agave nectar

¼ ounce Monin Mango Premium
    Gourmet syrup

3 blackberries

5 blueberries

1½ ounces fresh pineapple juice

½ ounce freshly squeezed orange
    juice

GARNISH 3 fresh blueberries

Combine the first six ingredients in a large shaking tin. Muddle the berries five or six times. Add the pineapple juice and orange juice, and ice to fill. Shake vigorously, then pour into a double-rocks glass. Top drink with three fresh blueberries.

THE LUDA (LUDACRIS) MARTINI

MAKES 1 COCKTAIL

1 ounce Conjure Cognac

½ ounce Cointreau liqueur

½ ounce Grand Marnier liqueur

½ ounce simple syrup, plus more for
   rim of glass

1 ounce freshly squeezed orange
   juice

GARNISH sugar for glass rim, crescent
   slice of orange

Combine all of the ingredients except the garnishes in a large shaking tin. Add 10 to 12 ounces ice. Shake vigorously twelve to fourteen times. Coat the rim of a chilled martini glass with the simple syrup, then dip the rim into sugar. Strain the cocktail into the glass, and garnish with the orange crescent to serve.

TUSCAN LEMONADE

MAKES 1 COCKTAIL

¾ ounce Hendrick's gin

¾ ounce St. Germain liqueur

½ ounce simple syrup

1 ounce fresh sour mix

3 sprigs fresh basil

2 ounces club soda or San Pellegrino

GARNISH 1 lemon wheel, 1 basil leaf

Combine all of the ingredients except the soda and garnish in a large shaking tin. Muddle the contents five or six times. Add 9 ounces ice, and shake vigorously. Pour the contents into a high-ball glass filled with ice. Top with club soda or San Pellegrino. Hang a lemon wheel on the side of the glass, and float a basil leaf.

YO CUZ MARTINI

MAKES 1 COCKTAIL

2 ounces Stolichnaya Elit vodka

GARNISH 3 olives stuffed with either
Maytag blue cheese, hot red
pepper, or black truffle

Pour the vodka into a large shaking tin with 10 ounces ice. Shake ten to twelve times. Strain into a chilled martini glass. Pick the guest's choice of olives, and place in the cocktail.

YO CUZ!

MOVING FORWARD

I DON'T KNOW WHAT SUCCESS MEANS OR LOOKS LIKE. People talk about success like it's magic—as if it appears out of thin air. Or they talk like success is something lasting—once you've got it, you can never lose it. I've never known either to be true. However, I do know this: if you want to do well in life, you need to approach every single day like it's a heavyweight fight. You get up in the morning, put on your gloves, and walk out the door throwing punches. And if you do that, day in and day out, you're going to win a lot more than you're going to lose. To me, that's what it's all about; in the restaurant business, you have to prove your-self again and again and again. You're only as good as your last meal. My macaroni is my uppercut. My meatball's my knockout punch. My canno-li's . . . well, you get the picture.

> **If you want to do well in life, you need to approach every single day like it's a heavyweight fight.**

That sense of urgency motivates me today, just like it did when I first opened Cafe Martorano in Fort Lauderdale. When we got started, I really had just $40 to my name. I couldn't let this restaurant fail. After buying the restaurant and a small house, we didn't even have any money left over for furniture. Debbie and I and our two boys, Joey and Steven, were sleeping on the floor. When we watched TV or ate, we sat on plastic beach chairs. The only real furniture in the house was a bedroom set that belonged to my mother, who was living with us.

A week after we opened, I decided to head a few blocks up the street, near the high-end hotels, and drum up business for Cafe Martorano. Against Debbie's wishes, I took $20 from the cash register and went to a classy club nearby called Septembers. I ordered the cheapest thing I could find—a $3 glass of white wine—and nursed the thing. When I finished it, I

ABOVE *Cafe Martorano staff*

We've built a reputation on word of mouth from day one.

went into the bathroom and filled the glass with water. The entire night, I told anyone who'd listen about this great new restaurant down the street, Cafe Martorano. Then, before the club closed, I tipped the bartender the remaining $17, asked if he wouldn't mind sending customers to my new place, and told him to stop by for a free glass of wine.

I did that a lot in those first few years and got great referrals from the local bartenders and waitresses. Seventeen-dollar tips here and there bought a lot of goodwill. I learned that trick from my father, who was always great at that kind of thing. I created my own small breaks, but sometimes they led to really big ones that I could have never imagined.

In 1993, just about a year after we opened, Tony Bennett and his crew dined with us one night before a concert. His assistant had heard good things about our place from a bartender at one of those nightclubs where I'd tipped big on a cheap glass of white wine.

I'll never forget that night. That was a first for me. I'd cooked for wiseguys before, but never a celebrity. The funny thing was that when I came out of the kitchen to meet Bennett and his group, I almost walked past them—I didn't recognize him right away. But then he stood up, extended his hand, and introduced himself. I made him orecchiette with broccoli rabe. And I knew I did a great job, because even though Tony Bennett was my first celebrity, he wasn't my last. Five years after we first opened, NFL great Joe Montana flew me out to his Napa Valley estate to cook for eight hundred guests for his annual charity benefit. Five years after that, I found myself cooking for the entire cast of *The Sopranos* at the Foxwoods Resort Casino in Connecticut. And now I'm cooking for another generation of superstars: Ludacris, Jamie Foxx, CeeLo, Ben Affleck, Matt Damon, Tom Brady and his teammates from the New England Patriots, Dwyane Wade. The list goes on and on. Heck, a few years ago Jimmy Kimmel even had me to his home in L.A. to watch Sunday football. I think I spent more time cooking than watching the game, but what a great experience—I wouldn't have had it any other way.

One thing always just led to another. I think the reason these opportunities came my way—the reason we were able to stay open in the early days and eventually grow to five restaurants—is that we've been consistently good. We've built a reputation on word of mouth from day one. We've never advertised. Hell, we don't even answer the phone a lot of times. That's no joke.

> **I want to give you my best. That's my fight. That's the reason I get up, morning after morning.**

Whether you are Hall of Famer Joe Montana or a just an average Joe, I want to give you my best. That's my fight. That's the reason I get up, morning after morning. Is that *success*? You tell me, cuz.

EVER SINCE I LEARNED TO COOK, quality has been at the forefront of what I do. Customers have always appreciated that. But I think the really good things came our way when I started being true to myself—where I came from, what I was about, the things I knew.

For example, back in Philly, whenever I fooled with a restaurant con-

ABOVE *With Joe Montana*

cept in which I was trying to be something I wasn't, it failed. But when I stuck to South Philly–style comfort food, people went nuts, because it was authentic. It was a part of me.

I expanded on that idea in the late 1990s. In 1997, I bought the storefront next to mine and doubled the size of Cafe Martorano. I used the extra space to build a DJ booth and outfitted the restaurant with big-ass speakers, Martin lights, and, of course, a mirror ball. Why not combine my two loves? To me, music and food had always gone together. Plus, I was once a damn good DJ in my glory days. Why couldn't I be both a DJ *and* a cook? I didn't see a reason why not. While I was at it, I decided I was going to show movies–stuff like *The Godfather* and others I loved–like I did back at Anton's in South Philly. When I worked with my father at the bar, that idea had been a hit. So, along with the sound equipment, I went about adding a bunch of TVs to the place. No one was doing this kind of thing at the time, but I wasn't going to let that stop me.

Before I knew it, Cafe Martorano had taken on my personality, and we went from being a hidden gem to having a line out the door every night. People knew it was a place for a great meal and a great time.

We expanded again in 2003, and with that growth came more attention, bigger crowds, and new celebrities. I've always tried to treat everyone the same, so celebrities waited in line just like everyone else. Some were great about it. Some weren't. But what can you do?

One night in the early days of Cafe Martorano, word got back to the kitchen that the now late, great Bruno Kirby was in the parking lot with Lynn, his wife, waiting for a table. (I loved him as young Clemenza in *The Godfather II*.) I always felt guilty that I had only a dozen or so tables in the restaurant then, so, in order to make the wait for a table a little more bearable, I'd send free appetizers outside to the customers in line. That night, I sent out some of my famous meatballs, even though the couple were vegetarians and told me they hadn't eaten meat in something like ten years.

"Well, that's it," Bruno said. "I'm no longer a vegetarian. I just had to have one–and then another. The best meatball I've ever had." We even took a picture of him eating one on the hood of a car.

ABOVE *Shaquille O'Neal*

Another time, Madonna left in a huff because we had a packed house and a three-hour wait. I didn't have the heart to tell her that the reason she couldn't be seated was that another celebrity with an entourage had beaten her to the punch: Steven Tyler of Aerosmith.

I'VE ALWAYS APPRECIATED THE ATTENTION we've gotten from great entertainers and ballplayers, but the one customer I was proudest to serve was my uncle Raymond.

He was released from prison in November 1999, when his conviction was overturned. He had spent seventeen years in prison, and shortly after he became a free man, we held a homecoming party for him at Cafe Martorano. The night my uncle walked through that door with my aunt Evelyn, it was like a celebrity had come to the restaurant. He had done a long stretch and didn't rat on anyone, staying true to the things he believed in. Everyone was excited and in the mood to celebrate, but we kept things low-key. At the end of the night, we sat down together and had a drink.

"I'm very proud of you, my nephew," he said.

It ended up being a bittersweet moment, because just a few years later, he became a marked man.

> The one customer I was proudest to serve was my uncle Raymond.

In January 2002, as Uncle Raymond was driving to a doctor's appointment, someone put three bullets through his car windshield, hitting Uncle Raymond in the arm, chest, and stomach. That tough son of a bitch tried driving himself to the hospital with half of his arm hanging off while he was bleeding his guts out.

A few weeks after he was shot, Uncle Raymond passed away. He was seventy-four.

When I heard the news, I went into the bathroom and looked in the mirror. *Uncle Raymond did his time and kept his mouth shut, and this was the thanks he got?* I knew this was the life he chose, and I reminded myself that I wasn't my uncle. I loved him like a father and mourned his death, but left it at that. I was on my own path, one that had taken me out of South Philly and the dead ends. There was no turning back. I knew what I wanted and, more important, what I had to do. It was a turning point for me. A way to finally move on.

ABOVE *With my trainer, Angel*

IN SOUTH PHILLY, the Martorano name had always been respected, but I was out to turn it into something respectable–legitimate–on a larger scale. To that end, we expanded a third time, in the early 2000s, on Oakland Park Boulevard, and started to get national renown to go along with the swelling crowds.

One night in 2005, we had a nice crowd but were not overly busy, and seven people walked in. They asked me to cook for them. I approached the table, and I gave my spiel.

"The stuff you get here, you're not gonna get anywhere else. I'll start you out with a Philly cheesesteak–homestyle, like my mother would make–and some chicken wings done in a special sauce that will blow your minds. Then we'll go with an Italian hoagie, a pizza, and, of course, my meatballs."

"Just keep the food coming," they said.

After the appetizers and about three pasta dishes, they threw in the towel.

I found out later that the guy who brought in the group was Marvin Shanken, the owner and publisher of the magazines *Cigar Aficionado* and

"Steve Martorano may just make the best meatball in the world." —*Gourmet*

ABOVE *Hard Rock kitchen staff in Hollywood, Florida*

Wine Spectator. Later, he sent me a letter asking if he could do a review of the restaurant in *Cigar Aficionado*.

To me, that was a big deal. I later found out that Shanken never did reviews, so I was touched that he picked Cafe Martorano for his first. Great article. Great publicity. Stuff like that really helped put us on the map. We've had a lot of reviews over the years—and, to tell the truth, most of them get my balls twisted for one reason or another—but I appreciated the *Cigar Aficionado* review because the guy who wrote it really knew food. Not long after that, we got another great plug when a writer from *Gourmet* magazine wrote, "Steve Martorano may just make the best meatball in the world."

Public praise and good reviews from respected writers are great, but, honestly, nothing means more to me than when someone from the old neighborhood comes in and says, "My mom's was good, but yours is better."

In 2007, the one opportunity I'd been waiting for my whole life came, that chance to be the best: Vegas.

The big league.

It was almost the end of me, though.

ABOVE *Paris Hotel staff, Las Vegas*

Martorano's Las Vegas at the Rio All-Suites Hotel and Casino was an uphill battle from the very beginning. The hotel is off the Strip, meaning that, unless they were staying at the Rio, customers would have to go out of their way to find us. To complicate matters, the space for the new restaurant was in the back of the casino, and the space itself was huge, seven thousand square feet. So it was like this giant, hidden restaurant next to the penny slots—the worst spot in the casino.

Then there were problems with the staff. I had brought a lot of my guys from Cafe Martorano in Fort Lauderdale to Vegas to help launch the new venture. But some of the guys weren't willing to put in the work and were disappointed to find out the place wasn't going to be an overnight smash. Meanwhile, others saw the time in Vegas as a party trip rather than a business one. They'd stay up all night, gamble, and drink, then show up late for work. And they were spending more than they were making. It was a recipe for disaster.

So I ended up firing some guys. I did a lot of soul-searching and didn't sleep much. I also watched *Rocky Balboa*, with Sylvester Stallone, on my hotel-room TV. "It ain't about how hard you hit," I listened to Rocky tell his son, "it's about how hard you can get hit and keep moving forward—

how much you can take and keep moving forward. That's how winning is done." The words spoke to me. They reminded me of everything I'd been through and all I wanted to accomplish. I swear I watched the movie again and again, night after night for eight months. I knew it word for word.

It's kind of funny the way little things like that get you through the day, but stuff like watching *Rocky Balboa* and listening to Sam Cooke's "A Change Is Gonna Come" helped pull me up and face the next day. Every night that fucking place brought me to my knees—I never knew if I was going to be cooking for one or one thousand—but I took it day by day, punch by punch.

In the end, we got it figured it out, and the restaurant became a success. Look, any jerk-off can take a restaurant that's in a brand-new hotel with high rollers on the Strip and make it into something respectable. That's no trick—people do it all the time. But since we opened in the Rio, we've been pulling people from other hotels to our out-of-the-way location. I don't know many other restaurants that could do that, or chefs who'd put in the work to make that happen. It takes balls, and I'm proud of that accomplishment.

We learned a lot from the Rio experience, and it opened doors for us.

In 2010, I opened a third restaurant, at the Seminole Hard Rock Hotel and Casino in Hollywood, Florida. We've done some innovative things at Martorano's Italian-American Kitchen, like opening a mozzarella bar and offering blackjack tables inside the restaurant. And in 2014, we're opening Martorano's at the Paris Hotel and Casino Las Vegas and at Harrah's hotel and casino in Atlantic City. This restaurant—with more than two hundred seats—is in the hotel's Le Boulevard shopping and dining area, by one of Gordon Ramsay's places. It's a great location. I finally made it to the Strip, but don't plan to rest there. We'll see. I'm always on the lookout for opportunities, whether they mean doing something unique or expanding.

But, no matter what, I know it all begins and ends with food.

It's funny—you see some restaurants go up, and guys want to spend

> **"It ain't about how hard you hit, it's about how hard you can get hit . . . and keep moving forward. That's how winning is done."**

ABOVE *Me and Tom Angelo signing the Atlantic City deal*

thousands on tile and mirrors and chandeliers, but pay a line cook just $9 a hour. Don't get me wrong, I want a great-looking place. But I'm more interested in paying that line cook $20 an hour, because, in the end, his work is what people are paying for.

Decorations can only carry you so far. Your food better be great, or your restaurant is going to fail. Back when I was selling hoagies out of my mother's basement, people didn't care that I was making their sandwiches in a row house; they cared what it tasted like. I've never forgotten that. I'm willing to fail—sometimes you learn a lot by doing something wrong—but I'm not going to fail because what I put on the plate isn't any good. That's unacceptable.

COMPETING IN THIS BUSINESS night in and night out isn't easy, and there's often a price to be paid, whether it comes at the expense of your health or your relationships. In my case, it's been both.

ABOVE *Me and Marsha*

About the time I opened at the Rio, I started having chest pains. I thought it might have something to do with weight lifting, which I do almost every day. But when I went to see my doctor in Fort Lauderdale, he told me it was my heart. Ninety-eight percent of three of the major arteries leading to my heart were clogged, includ-ing one called "the widow maker." I had surgery and got things cleaned up, but I was sidelined for weeks, prompting rumors that my place in the Rio was going to close. Shutting down never crossed my mind; if anything, the experience with my heart made me a stronger, more determined person. Just like my father, a person can drop dead at any minute. If that happens, so be it. I just want to make sure I make the most out of every second I've got.

I just want to make sure I make the most out of every second I've got.

For a while, I wasn't doing that.

Even though I left Philly to get away from a certain lifestyle, I went through periods in my life when I was hooking up with the same crowd, doing some of the same dumb things I did as a kid.

At one point, even after working all day, I'd stay out all night, drinking and partying and getting high. I was in a downward spiral. My marriage wasn't the best, either. Debbie and I were together for a long time, and I'm grateful that she helped me get to a certain point. She's a great, great mother, and we raised two wonderful kids. Still, people change, and we wound up getting divorced.

During one of the worst periods of my life, I was fortunate that one night Marsha Daley walked into my restaurant. I remember her stand-ing by the wall as she waited for an open table. I walked up to her and explained that it might be a couple of hours before something opened up. She looked at me like I had five heads, so I found her a spot at the bar and fed her. I wasn't looking for anything, but that meeting ended up being the start of a relationship that's lasted for almost a decade.

Marsha's a beautiful Jamaican woman who is a professional makeup artist, but underneath that gorgeous exterior lies a real toughness. She's the one who'd come and pull me out of nightclubs at five or six in the morning and set me straight. She's the one who pointed out that I was getting high and partying with guys I didn't even really know, and that I was poised to lose everything I'd worked so hard for. Then she told me I was going to lose her if I didn't get my shit together, and from that moment on, I've been clean.

Marsha saved me, as much as food did.

That experience has made me realize I don't just want to succeed, I want to make a difference. And I don't mean just with food or in business. I mean with people.

I DIDN'T HAVE A VISION OR A DREAM when I began cooking. Really, I was just trying to pay the bills and survive. But, over the years, what I started has become a brand. It's kind of like having a baby who grows up in ways you can't imagine. Now the name Martorano stands for Italian-American food and tradition and a fun experience–all under one roof. We've gone from one restaurant to a second, and then a third, and a fourth, and maybe more. I could continue to grow in that way (and probably will), but other things interest me, too.

I don't just want to succeed, I want to make a difference.

I've always loved TV, and a cooking show seems like a natural way to go. In fact, I've been a guest on a number of shows over the years.

One of my favorite experiences was on *The Mo'Nique Show*. I was just expecting to cook, but she actually had me sit on the couch and tell my story. That was it–no cooking. She just wanted to hear my story. That blew me away, and my appearance seemed to have an impact on others. You can't believe the response I got from people in the social media. There were letters and phone calls, too. I heard from one person in Africa who wanted to be doctor, another who wanted to be a lawyer. They were looking to me for encouragement and inspiration. That really got me thinking.

So what I do now is try to get people to see food as a vehicle for change and opportunity. I spend a good deal of my time in schools with at-risk kids, and visit guys in prison. I know what it feels like to come from circumstances where the only options you have are bad ones. I hope that when I speak to them–or teach them how to cook–they may see what I've been able to do and use that as an example. Look, if I can do it, they can, too. And it doesn't even have to be food or cooking. The big idea is not to let anyone tell them what they can or can't be. That's up to them to decide.

Or maybe–at same point through a cooking show or now through this book–I can make a difference in other ways. Maybe it's teaching the mom who works all day, and then comes home and has to feed her husband and kids on a budget, that making great food is within reach. Maybe it's also teaching that mom–or her husband–that you don't have to have a lot of time or money to bring your family together over a bowl of out-of-this-world pasta. It worked in South Philly when I was growing up, and it'll work in your home, too.

But, no matter who you are, you can't quit or give up. And, yeah, it might be a struggle and a fight, but it's worth it. You're worth it, cuz.

I was, too.

We all are.

Fighters fight, cuz!

ACKNOWLEDGMENTS

First, I want to thank God for never giving up on me.

I never thought about writing a book. I never liked homework. Writing a book about my life never occurred to me until one day someone told me, I have been following your career for a very long time, I have seen your struggles and how you have overcome the odds, and never gave up. You succeeded, your story changed my life. At that very moment, I realized I had a lot to share.

It's true what they say, "Life is all about relationships." If it were not for my relationships with a group of special people in my life, this would all still be a dream. I want to thank Ben Frosch who kicked off this journey by introducing me to Ken Aguado. Ken became the producer for my cooking show, a major pain in my ass, but mostly a great friend. Ken introduced me to my late entertainment attorney, Ed Lassman. Ed passed away suddenly before this book was published, but I know he's smiling down on me. Ed introduced me to my now agent, Jonathan Russo of Artists Agency, who was not taking on any new clients at the time but believed I had something to share with the world and took me on anyway. Jonathan introduced me to Janis Donnaud, my book agent. She never takes no for an answer. Thanks to all of you for being in my life and making this possible.

Janis, this would never have been possible without you. You believed in me more than I believed in myself at times. You knew I had a story to tell and you never stopped until it was told. Janis introduced me to Peter Gethers at Random House. Peter Gethers, thank you for taking my book to another level and going beyond measure to make sure everything was impeccable.

Thank you Caesars Entertainment, the Rio All Suite Las Vegas Hotel and Casino, and the Seminole Hard Rock Hotel and Casino for believing in a neighborhood guy from the streets of South Philadelphia.

Thank you to my mother, Lillian Martorano; she's eighty-five and still tells me what to do and how to cook. Thank you to my attorney, Tom Angelo, for always having my back; my trainer, Angel, for always making sure I'm in my best shape. My dear late friend Frank Potenza, aka Uncle Frank, I know your spirit is with me always. Thank you to my managers and staff at Cafe Martorano in Fort Lauderdale, Florida; Martorano's Italian-American Kitchen in Hollywood, Florida; and at Martorano's Las Vegas.

A special thank-you to Ken and Nina Stowe. Thank you for always lifting me up when I am down and always reminding me **THE BEST IS YET TO COME.**

Lastly, to my best friend, Marsha Daley, no words can truly express what you mean to me. I might not be able to get you that mansion on the hill but I'll make you my queen forever. 'Cause the first time I saw you I was in heaven. I love you, kid.

INDEX

(Page references in *italics* refer to illustrations.)

Truffle Oil, Prosciutto-Wrapped
Pappardelle with Cream and, 70,
70, 71
tubetti, in Pasta with Peas and
Onion, 72
Tuna, Fresh, with Whole-Wheat
Spaghetti, 110
Tuscan Lemonade, 148, *149*
Twisted Berry Cocktail, 145
Tyler, Steven, 157

U

Umbertos Clam House, New York, 59

V

Valentino's, Cherry Hill, N.J.,
81–82, *82*
veal:
Cutlet Insalata, 16
Cutlet Marsala, 92
Parmesan Sandwich, 17
Piccata, *112*, 113
Sinatra, 111
Stuffed Hot Peppers, *10*, 37
substituting pork for, 16
Veev Açai Spirit liqueur, in Twisted Berry
Cocktail, 145
vinegar, red-wine, 15

vodka:
Black Beauty Martini, 136, *137*
Cosmo Bianco, *138*, 139
Crystal Grape Martini, 140,
141
Harvest Peach Martini, *142*, 143
Sauce, Penne and, 62
Sicilian Mule, 144
Simply Red Martini, 145
Yo Cuz Martini, *150*, 151

W

Wade, Dwyane, 155
Watermelon Arugula Salad, 12
Whole-Wheat Spaghetti, Fresh Tuna
with, 110
Wild Mushroom Sauté, The
Gink's, 38
Wings Bibz Style, 39

Y

Yo Cuz Martini, *150*, 151

Z

zabaglione:
with Berries, 132, *133*
Peanut Butter, Peanut Butter Cake
with, 131

A NOTE ABOUT THE AUTHOR

Steve Martorano is the owner of Cafe Martorano in Fort Lauderdale and Hollywood, Florida, two Martorano's locations in Las Vegas, Nevada, and one in Atlantic City, New Jersey. He has also launched a Martorano wine label, pasta sauces, and a line of clothing. He currently resides in Fort Lauderdale.

A NOTE ON THE TYPE

This book was set in Bodoni, a typeface named after Giambattista Bodoni (1740–1813), the celebrated printer and type designer of Parma. Bodoni's types featured greater contrast in the thick and thin elements and a sharper and more angular finish of details. The Bodoni types of today are a modern version of the Bodoni manner.

COMPOSED BY NORTH MARKET STREET GRAPHICS, LANCASTER, PENNSYLVANIA

PRINTED AND BOUND BY LEE FUNG PRINTERS, CHINA

DESIGNED BY MAGGIE HINDERS